180 Days of PRACTICE

GRADE
5

HANDS-ON
STEAM

| Science | Technology | Engineering | Arts | Mathematics |

...all ingredients until they are combined. Mix everything with your hands until it is not sticky. Then add in the glitter.

What concerns do you have about your design?
My concern is that the slime will be too runny.

12   © Shell Education

29648—180 Days: Hands-On STEAM

Kristin Kemp, M.A.Ed.

Publishing Credits

Corinne Burton, M.A.Ed., *Publisher*
Emily R. Smith, M.A.Ed., *VP of Content Development*
Véronique Bos, *Creative Director*
Lynette Ordoñez, *Content Manager*
Melissa Laughlin, *Editor*
Jill Malcolm, *Graphic Designer*
David Slayton, *Assistant Editor*

Image Credits: all images Shutterstock and/or iStock

Standards

NGSS Lead States. 2013. *Next Generation Science Standards: For States, By States.* Washington, DC: The National Academies Press.
© 2021 TESOL International Association
© 2021 Board of Regents of the University of Wisconsin System

A division of Teacher Created Materials
5482 Argosy Avenue
Huntington Beach, CA 92649
www.tcmpub.com/shell-education
ISBN 978-1-4258-2532-4
© 2022 Shell Educational Publishing, Inc.
Printed in USA. WOR004

Table of Contents

Introduction

    Research..4

        The Importance of STEAM Education 4

        Defining STEAM 5

        The Engineering Design Process. 6

        How to Facilitate Successful STEAM Challenges...................7

    How to Use This Resource............................9

        Unit Structure Overview 9

        Pacing Options 10

        Teaching Support Pages 11

        Student Pages 12

        Assessment Options 14

    Standards Correlations 15

180 Days of Practice

    Physical Science

        Unit 1: Chemical Reactions..........................17

        Unit 2: Gravity.....................................34

        Unit 3: Mixtures and Solutions 51

        Unit 4: Properties of Matter 68

    Life Science

        Unit 5: Bones and Skeletons 85

        Unit 6: Decomposers 102

        Unit 7: Living in Extremes..........................119

        Unit 8: Primary Producers..........................136

    Earth and Space Science

        Unit 9: Earth in Motion 153

        Unit 10: Hurricanes................................170

        Unit 11: Sun and Stars 187

        Unit 12: Water on Earth 204

    Appendixes

    STEAM Challenge Rubric............................221

    Summative Assessment 222

    Engineering Design Process 223

    Digital Resources..................................224

    References Cited 224

Research

The Importance of STEAM Education

STEAM education is a powerful approach to learning that continues to gain momentum and support across the globe. STEAM is the integration of science, technology, engineering, the arts, and mathematics to design solutions for real-world problems. Students must learn how to question, explore, and analyze natural phenomena. With these skills in hand, students understand the complexity of available information and are empowered to become independent learners and problem solvers.

The content and practices of STEAM education are strong components of a balanced instructional approach, ensuring students are college- and career-ready. The application of STEAM practices in the classroom affords teachers opportunities to challenge students to apply new knowledge. Students of all ages can design and build structures, improve existing products, and test innovative solutions to real-world problems. STEAM instruction can be as simple as using recycled materials to design a habitat for caterpillars discovered on the playground and as challenging as designing a solution to provide clean water to developing countries. The possibilities are endless.

Blending arts principles with STEM disciplines prepares students to be problem solvers, creative collaborators, and thoughtful risk-takers. Even students who do not choose a career in a STEAM field will benefit because these skills can be translated into almost any career. Students who become STEAM proficient are prepared to answer complex questions, investigate global issues, and develop solutions for real-world challenges. Rodger W. Bybee (2013, 64) summarizes what is expected of students as they join the workforce:

> As literate adults, individuals should be competent to understand STEM-related global issues; recognize scientific from other nonscientific explanations; make reasonable arguments based on evidence; and, very important, fulfill their civic duties at the local, national, and global levels.

Likewise, STEAM helps students understand how concepts are connected as they gain proficiency in the Four Cs: creativity, collaboration, critical thinking, and communication.

Research *(cont.)*

Defining STEAM

STEAM is an integrated way of preparing students for the twenty-first century world. It places an emphasis on understanding science and mathematics while learning engineering skills. By including art, STEAM recognizes that the creative aspect of any project is integral to good design—whether designing an experiment or an object.

Science

Any project or advancement builds on prior science knowledge. Science focuses on learning and applying specific content, cross-cutting concepts, and scientific practices that are relevant to the topic or project.

Technology

This is what results from the application of scientific knowledge and engineering. It is something that is created to solve a problem or meet a need. Some people also include the *use* of technology in this category. That is, tools used by scientists and engineers to solve problems. In addition to computers and robots, technology can include nets used by marine biologists, anemometers used by meteorologists, computer software used by mathematicians, and so on.

Engineering

This is the application of scientific knowledge to meet a need, solve a problem, or address phenomena. For example, engineers design bridges to withstand huge loads. Engineering is also used to understand phenomena, such as in designing a way to test a hypothesis. When problems arise, such as those due to earthquakes or rising sea levels, engineering is required to design solutions to the problems. On a smaller scale, a homeowner might want to find a solution to their basement flooding.

Art

In this context, art equals creativity and creative problem-solving. For example, someone might want to test a hypothesis but be stumped as to how to set up the experiment. Perhaps you have a valuable painting. You think there is another valuable image below the first layer of paint on the canvas. You do not want to destroy the painting on top. A creative solution is needed. Art can also include a creative or beautiful design that solves a problem. For example, the Golden Gate Bridge is considered both an engineering marvel and a work of art.

Mathematics

This is the application of mathematics to real-world problems. Often, this includes data analysis—such as collecting data, graphing it, analyzing the data, and then communicating that analysis. It may also include taking mathematical measurements in the pursuit of an answer. The idea is not to learn new math, but rather to apply it; however, some mathematics may need to be learned to solve the specific problem. Isaac Newton, for example, is famous for *inventing* calculus to help him solve problems in understanding gravity and motion.

Research *(cont.)*

The Engineering Design Process

The most essential component of STEAM education is the engineering design process. This process is an articulated approach to problem solving in which students are guided through the iterative process of solving problems and refining solutions to achieve the best possible outcomes. There are many different versions of the engineering design process, but they all have the same basic structure and goals. As explained in Appendix I of NGSS (2013), "At any stage, a problem-solver can redefine the problem or generate new solutions to replace an idea that just isn't working out."

Each unit in this resource presents students with a design challenge in an authentic and engaging context. The practice pages guide and support students through the engineering design process to solve problems or fulfill needs.

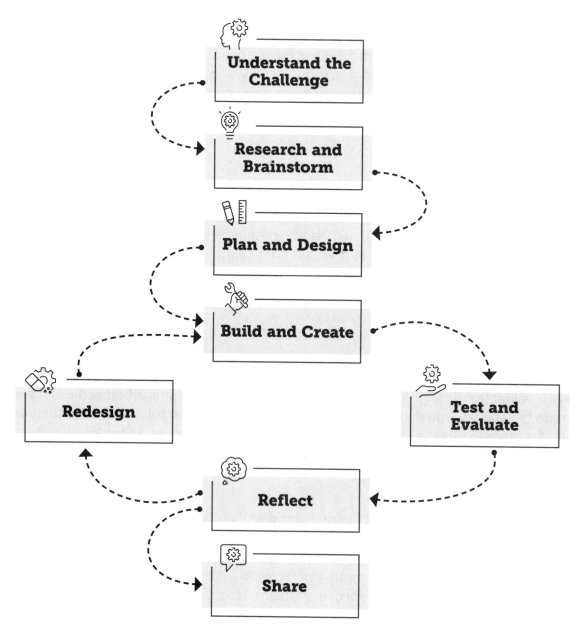

Research *(cont.)*

How to Facilitate Successful STEAM Challenges

There are some basic rules to remember as your students complete STEAM challenges.

Both independent and collaborative work should be included.

Astronaut and inventor Ellen Ochoa is well-known for working a robotic arm in space. About that experience she said, "It's fun to work the robotic arm, in part because it's a team effort." She recognized that she was getting credit for something amazing that happened because of the collaborative work of hundreds of people.

Students need time to think through a project, both on their own and together with others. It is often best to encourage students to start by thinking independently. One student may think of a totally different solution than another student. Once they come together, students can merge aspects of each other's ideas to devise something even better.

Failure is a step in the process.

During the process of trying to invent a useful light bulb, Thomas Edison famously said, "I have not failed. I've just found 10,000 ways that won't work." People are innovating when they are failing because it is a chance to try something new. The STEAM challenges in this book intentionally give students chances to improve their designs. Students should feel free to innovate as much as possible, especially the first time around. Then, they can build on what they learned and try again.

Some students get stuck thinking there is one right way. There are almost always multiple solutions to a problem. For example, attaching train cars together used to be very dangerous. In the late nineteenth century, different solutions to this problem were invented in England and the United States to make the process safer. Both solutions worked, and both were used! Encourage students to recognize that there are usually different ways to solve problems. Discuss the pros and cons of the various solutions that students generate.

Research *(cont.)*

How to Facilitate Successful STEAM Challenges *(cont.)*

Getting inspiration from others is an option.

Students worry a lot about copying. It is important to remind them that all breakthroughs come on the shoulders of others. No one is working in a vacuum, and it is okay to get inspiration and ideas from others. It is also important to give credit to the people whose work and ideas inspired others. Students may see this as cheating, but they should be encouraged to see that they had a great enough idea that others recognized it and wanted to build on it.

The struggle is real—and really important.

Most people do not like to fail. And it can be frustrating not to know what to do or what to try next. Lonnie Johnson, engineer and toy inventor, advises, "Persevere. That's what I always say to people. There's no easy route." Try to support students during this struggle, as amazing innovations can emerge from the process. Further, students feel great when they surprise themselves with success after thinking they were not going to succeed.

Materials can inspire the process.

Students may be stumped about how they are going to build a boat…until you show them that they can use clay. A parachute is daunting, but a pile of tissue paper or plastic bags might suddenly make students feel like they have some direction. On the other hand, materials can also instantly send the mind in certain directions, without exploring other options. For this reason, consider carefully the point at which you want to show students the materials they can use. You might want them to brainstorm materials first. This might inspire you to offer materials you had not considered before.

Some students or groups will need different types of support.

If possible, have students who need additional support manipulate materials, play with commercial solutions, or watch videos to get ideas. For students who need an additional challenge, consider ways to make the challenge more "real world" by adding additional realistic criteria. Or, encourage students to add their own criteria.

How to Use This Resource

Unit Structure Overview

This resource is organized into 12 units. Each three-week unit is organized in a consistent format for ease of use.

Week 1: STEAM Content

Day 1 **Learn Content**	Students read text, study visuals, and answer multiple-choice questions.
Day 2 **Learn Content**	Students read text, study visuals, and answer short-answer questions.
Day 3 **Explore Content**	Students engage in hands-on activities, such as scientific investigations, mini building challenges, and drawing and labeling diagrams.
Day 4 **Get Creative**	Students use their creativity, imaginations, and artistic abilities in activities such as drawing, creating fun designs, and doing science-related crafts.
Day 5 **Analyze Data**	Students analyze and/or create charts, tables, maps, and graphs.

Week 2: STEAM Challenge

Day 1 **Understand the Challenge**	Students are introduced to the STEAM Challenge. They review the criteria and constraints for successful designs.
Day 2 **Research and Brainstorm**	Students conduct additional research, as needed, and brainstorm ideas for their designs.
Day 3 **Plan and Design**	Students plan and sketch their designs.
Day 4 **Build and Create**	Students use their materials to construct their designs.
Day 5 **Test and Evaluate**	Students conduct tests and/or evaluation to assess the effectiveness of their designs and how well they met the criteria of the challenge.

Week 3: STEAM Challenge Improvement

Day 1 **Reflect**	Students answer questions to reflect on their first designs and make plans for how to improve their designs.
Day 2 **Redesign**	Students sketch new or modified designs.
Day 3 **Rebuild and Refine**	Students rebuild or adjust their designs.
Day 4 **Retest**	Students retest and evaluate their new designs.
Day 5 **Reflect and Share**	Students reflect on their experiences working through the engineering design process. They discuss and share their process and results with others.

How to Use This Resource *(cont.)*

Pacing Options

This resource is flexibly designed and can be used in tandem with a core curriculum within a science, STEAM, or STEM block. It can also be used in makerspaces, after-school programs, summer school, or as enrichment activities at home. The following pacing options show suggestions for how to use this book.

Option 1

This option shows how each unit can be completed in 15 days. This option requires approximately 10–20 minutes per day. Building days are flexible, and teachers may allow for additional time at their discretion.

	Day 1	**Day 2**	**Day 3**	**Day 4**	**Day 5**
Week 1	Learn Content	Learn Content	Explore Content	Get Creative	Analyze Data
Week 2	Understand the Challenge	Research and Brainstorm	Plan and Design	Build and Create	Test and Evaluate
Week 3	Reflect	Redesign	Rebuild and Refine	Retest	Reflect and Share

Option 2

This option shows how each unit can be completed in fewer than 15 days. This option requires approximately 45–60 minutes a day.

	Day 1	**Day 2**
Week 1	Learn Content Explore Content	Get Creative Analyze Data
Week 2	Understand the Challenge Research and Brainstorm Plan and Design	Build and Create Test and Evaluate
Week 3	Reflect Redesign Rebuild and Refine	Retest Reflect and Share

How to Use This Resource *(cont.)*

Teaching Support Pages

Each unit in this resource begins with two teaching support pages that provide instructional guidance.

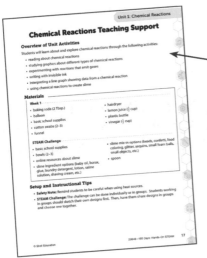

A clear overview of unit activities, weekly materials, safety notes, and setup tips helps teachers plan and prepare efficiently and with ease.

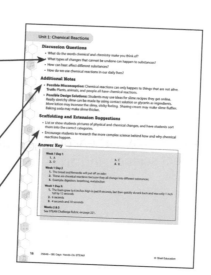

Discussion questions encourage students to verbalize their learning and connect it to their own lives.

Possible student misconceptions and design solutions further take the guesswork out of lesson planning.

Differentiation options offer ways to support and extend student learning.

Materials

Due to the nature of engineering, the materials listed are often flexible. They may be substituted or added to, depending on what you have available. More material options require greater consideration by students and encourage more creative and critical thinking. Fewer material options can help narrow students' focus but may limit creativity. Adjust the materials provided to fit the needs of your students.

Approximate amounts of materials are included in each list. These amount suggestions are per group. Students are expected to have basic school supplies for each unit. These include paper, pencils, markers or crayons, glue, tape, and scissors.

How to Use This Resource (cont.)

Student Pages

Students begin each unit by learning about and exploring science-related content.

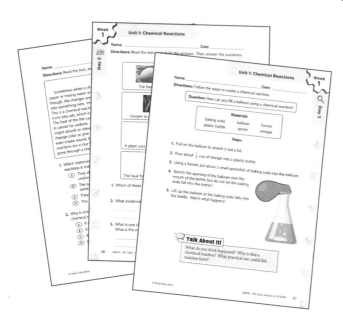

Activities in **Week 1** help build background science content knowledge relevant to the STEAM Challenge.

Creative activities encourage students to connect science and art.

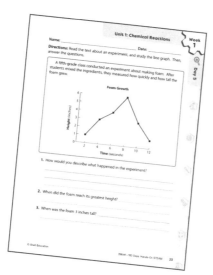

Graphs, charts, and maps guide students to make important mathematics and real-world connections.

How to Use This Resource *(cont.)*

Student Pages *(cont.)*

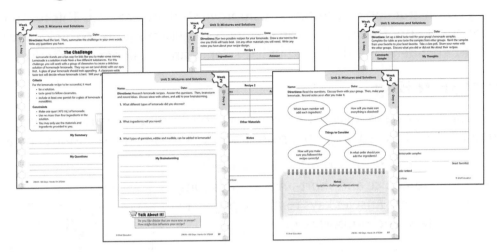

Week 2 introduces students to the STEAM Challenge. Activities guide students through each step of the engineering design process. They provide guiding questions and space for students to record their plans, progress, results, and thinking.

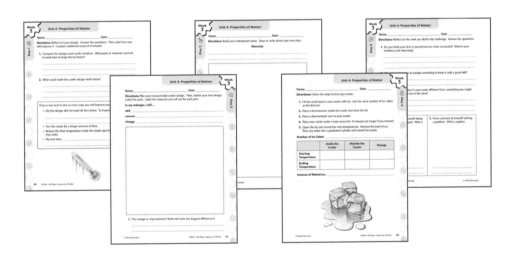

Week 3 activities continue to lead students through the cycle of the engineering design process. Students are encouraged to think about and discuss ways to improve their designs based on their observations and experiences in Week 2.

Quick Tip!

Staple all the student pages for each unit together, and distribute them as packets. This will allow students to easily refer to their learning as they complete the STEAM Challenges.

How to Use This Resource *(cont.)*

Assessment Options

Assessments guide instructional decisions and improve student learning. This resource offers balanced assessment opportunities. The assessments require students to think critically, respond to text-dependent questions, and utilize science and engineering practices.

Progress Monitoring

There are key points throughout each unit when valuable formative evaluations can be made. These evaluations can be based on group, paired, and/or individual discussions and activities.

- **Week 1** activities provide opportunities for students to answer multiple-choice and short-answer questions related to the content. Answer keys for these pages are provided in the Teaching Support pages.

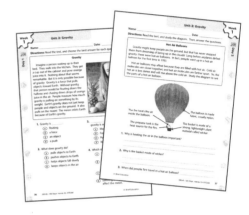

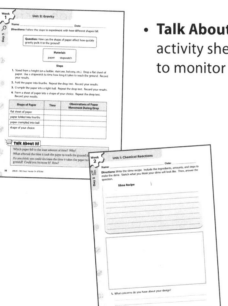

- **Talk About It!** graphics on student activity sheets offer opportunities to monitor student progress.

- **Week 2 Day 3: Plan and Design** is when students sketch their first designs. This is a great opportunity to assess how well students understand the STEAM challenge and what they plan to create. These should be reviewed before moving on to the Build and Create stages of the STEAM Challenges.

Summative Assessment

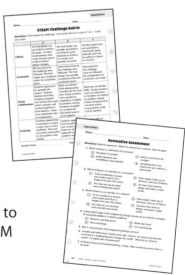

A rubric for the STEAM Challenges is provided on page 221. It is important to note that whether students' final designs were successful is not the main goal of this assessment. It is a way to assess students' skills as they work through the engineering design process. Students assess themselves first. Teachers can add notes to the assessment.

A short summative assessment is provided on page 222. This is meant to provide teachers with insight into how well students understand STEAM practices and the engineering design process.

Standards Correlations

Shell Education is committed to producing educational materials that are research and standards based. To support this effort, this resource is correlated to the academic standards of all 50 states, the District of Columbia, the Department of Defense Dependent Schools, and the Canadian provinces. A correlation is also provided for key professional educational organizations.

To print a customized correlation report for your state, visit our website at **www.tcmpub.com/ administrators/correlations** and follow the online directions. If you require assistance in printing correlation reports, please contact the Customer Service Department at 1-800-858-7339.

Standards Overview

The Every Student Succeeds Act (ESSA) mandates that all states adopt challenging academic standards that help students meet the goal of college and career readiness. While many states already adopted academic standards prior to ESSA, the act continues to hold states accountable for detailed and comprehensive standards. Standards are designed to focus instruction and guide adoption of curricula. They define the knowledge, skills, and content students should acquire at each level. Standards are also used to develop standardized tests to evaluate students' academic progress. State standards are used in the development of our resources, so educators can be assured they meet state academic requirements.

Next Generation Science Standards

This set of national standards aims to incorporate science knowledge and process standards into a cohesive framework. The standards listed on page 16 describe the science content and processes presented throughout the lessons.

TESOL and WIDA Standards

In this book, the following English language development standards are met: Standard 1: English language learners communicate for social and instructional purposes within the school setting. Standard 3: English language learners communicate information, ideas and concepts necessary for academic success in the content area of mathematics. Standard 4: English language learners communicate information, ideas and concepts necessary for academic success in the content area of science.

Standards Correlations (cont.)

Each unit in this resource supports all the following NGSS Scientific and Engineering Practices and Engineering Performance Expectations for 3–5.

Scientific and Engineering Practices	Engineering Performance Expectations
Asking Questions and Defining Problems	Define a simple design problem reflecting a need or a want that includes specified criteria for success and constraints on materials, time, or cost.
Developing and Using Models	
Planning and Carrying Out Investigations	
Analyzing and Interpreting Data	Generate and compare multiple possible solutions to a problem based on how well each is likely to meet the criteria and constraints of the problem.
Constructing Explanations and Designing Solutions	
Engaging in Argument from Evidence	Plan and carry out fair tests in which variables are controlled and failure points are considered to identify aspects of a model or prototype that can be improved.
Obtaining, Evaluating, and Communicating Information	

This chart shows how the units in this resource align to NGSS Disciplinary Core Ideas and Crosscutting Concepts.

Unit	Disciplinary Core Idea	Crosscutting Concept
Chemical Reactions	PS1.B: Chemical Reactions	Cause and Effect
Gravity	PS2.B: Types of Interactions	Cause and Effect
Mixtures and Solutions	PS1.A: Structure and Properties of Matter	Scale, Proportion, and Quantity
Properties of Matter	PS1.A: Structure and Properties of Matter	Scale, Proportion, and Quantity
Bones and Skeletons	LS4.D: Biodiversity and Humans	Cause and Effect
Decomposers	LS1.C: Organization for Matter and Energy Flow in Organisms LS2.A: Interdependent Relationships in Ecosystems LS2.B: Cycles of Matter and Energy Transfer in Ecosystems	Energy and Matter; Systems and System Models
Living in Extremes	LS1.A: Structure and Function LS1.C: Organization for Matter and Energy Flow in Organisms	Energy and Matter; Systems and System Models
Primary Producers	PS3.D: Energy in Chemical Processes and Everyday Life LS1.C: Organization for Matter and Energy Flow in Organisms	Energy and Matter; Systems and System Models
Earth in Motion	ESS1.B: Earth and the Solar System	Patterns
Hurricanes	ESS2.A: Earth Materials and Systems	Systems and System Models
Sun and Stars	ESS1.A: The Universe and Its Stars	Patterns; Scale, Proportion, and Quantity
Water on Earth	ESS2.C: The Roles of Water in Earth's Surface Processes	Scale, Proportion, and Quantity

Chemical Reactions Teaching Support

Overview of Unit Activities

Students will learn about and explore chemical reactions through the following activities:

- reading about chemical reactions
- studying graphics about different types of chemical reactions
- experimenting with reactions that emit gases
- writing with invisible ink
- interpreting a line graph showing data from a chemical reaction
- using chemical reactions to create slime

Materials Per Group

Week 1

- baking soda (2 tbsp., 29 g)
- balloon
- basic school supplies
- cotton swabs (2–3)
- funnel
- hairdryer
- lemon juice ($\frac{1}{2}$ cup, 125 mL)
- plastic bottle
- vinegar ($\frac{1}{2}$ cup, 125 mL)

STEAM Challenge

- basic school supplies
- bowls (2–3)
- online resources about slime
- slime ingredient options (baby oil, borax, glue, laundry detergent, lotion, saline solution, shaving cream, etc.)
- slime mix-in options (beads, confetti, food coloring, glitter, sequins, small foam balls, small objects, etc.)
- spoon

Setup and Instructional Tips

- **Safety Note:** Remind students to be careful when using heat sources.
- **STEAM Challenge:** The challenge can be done individually or in groups. Students working in groups should sketch their own designs first. Then, have them share designs in groups and choose one together.

Discussion Questions

- What do the words *chemical* and *chemistry* make you think of?
- What types of changes that cannot be undone can happen to substances?
- How can heat affect different substances?
- How do we use chemical reactions in our daily lives?

Additional Notes

- **Possible Misconception:** Chemical reactions can only happen to things that are not alive. **Truth:** Plants, animals, and people all have chemical reactions.
- **Possible Design Solutions:** Students may use ideas for slime recipes they get online. Really stretchy slime can be made by using contact solution or glycerin as ingredients. More lotion may increase the slimy, sticky feeling. Shaving cream may make slime fluffier. Baking soda may make slime thicker.

Scaffolding and Extension Suggestions

- List or show students pictures of physical and chemical changes, and have students sort them into the correct categories.
- Encourage students to research the more complex science behind how and why chemical reactions happen.

Answer Key

Week 1 Day 1
1. A
2. D
3. C
4. B

Week 1 Day 2
1. The bread and fireworks will put off an odor.
2. These are chemical reactions because they all change into different substances.
3. Example: digestion, breathing, metabolism

Week 1 Day 5:
1. The foam grew to 6 inches high in just 8 seconds, but then quickly shrunk back and was only 1 inch tall by 12 seconds.
2. 6 seconds
3. 4 seconds and 10 seconds

Weeks 2 & 3
See STEAM Challenge Rubric on page 221.

Name: _____ Date: _____

Directions: Read the text, and choose the best answer for each question.

Chemical Reactions

Sometimes when a change occurs to a substance, it is physical. Cutting paper or mixing water and sugar do not change the substances. Other times, though, the changes are chemical reactions, and substances are converted into something new. Imagine a piece of wood that catches on fire and burns. This is a chemical reaction because the wood turns into ash, which is a new substance. The heat of the fire caused the change, and it cannot be undone. Chemical reactions might absorb or release heat. They might change color or give off an odor. They might even create sound, light, or gas. Any of these reactions are a clue that a substance has gone through a chemical change.

1. Which statement about chemical reactions is true?
   - (A) They often cannot be undone.
   - (B) The substance stays the same.
   - (C) They do not give off odors.
   - (D) The reaction is silent.

2. Why is wood turning to ash a chemical reaction?
   - (A) It changes shape.
   - (B) It absorbs heat.
   - (C) It is a mixture.
   - (D) It becomes a new substance.

3. What causes the chemical reaction of wood turning to ash?
   - (A) light
   - (B) gas
   - (C) heat
   - (D) sound

4. Which of these is an example of a chemical reaction?
   - (A) slicing cheese
   - (B) baking cookies
   - (C) crumpling paper
   - (D) chopping wood

Day 1

Day 2

Name: _____ Date: _____

Directions: Read the text, and study the pictures. Then, answer the questions.

Chemical Reaction Examples

The heat of an oven bakes the dough into bread.

Oxygen (a gas) and water make a metal nail rust over time.

A plant uses carbon dioxide (a gas) and enzymes in soil to grow.

The heat from a firework's lit fuse causes it to explode in the sky.

1. Which of these chemical reaction(s) will give off an odor?

_____

2. What evidence is there that the above examples are chemical reactions?

_____

_____

3. What is one chemical reaction you can think of that happens in your body? What is the evidence that it is a chemical reaction?

_____

_____

Name: _____ Date: _____

Directions: Follow the steps to create a chemical reaction.

Question: How can you fill a balloon using a chemical reaction?

Materials

| baking soda | balloon | funnel |
| plastic bottle | spoon | vinegar |

Steps

1. Pull on the balloon to stretch it out a bit.

2. Pour about $\frac{1}{4}$ cup (60 mL) of vinegar into a plastic bottle.

3. Using a funnel, put about 2 small spoonfuls of baking soda into the balloon.

4. Stretch the opening of the balloon over the mouth of the bottle (but do not let the baking soda fall into the bottle!).

5. Lift up the balloon so the baking soda falls into the bottle. Watch what happens!

 Talk About It!

What do you think happened? Why is this a chemical reaction? What practical use could this reaction have?

Unit 1: Chemical Reactions

Name: _____ Date: _____

Directions: Dip a cotton swab in lemon juice. Draw a picture or write a message on the page. Let it dry, then use a lamp or hairdryer to heat up the paper and see what happens! It's a secret chemical reaction.

My Secret Message

Name: _____ Date: _____

Directions: Read the text about an experiment, and study the line graph. Then, answer the questions.

A fifth-grade class conducted an experiment about making foam. After students mixed the ingredients, they measured how quickly and how tall the foam grew.

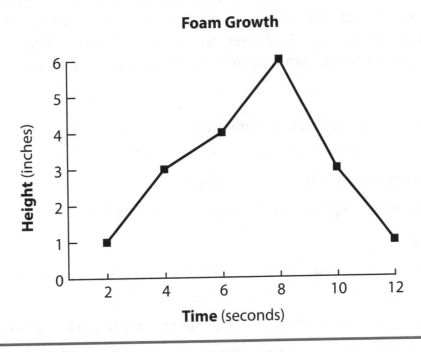

Foam Growth

1. How would you describe what happened in the experiment?

_____

_____

_____

2. When did the foam reach its greatest height? _____

_____

3. When was the foam 3 inches tall? _____

_____

Name: _____ Date: _____

Directions: Read the text. Then, summarize the challenge in your own words. Write any questions you have.

The Challenge

Mold it, shape it, squeeze it, stretch it—it's slime! Making homemade slime is a popular pastime. It's also a fun way to see chemical reactions firsthand. Some students make it for themselves; others decide to go into business or give it as gifts. And there are so many different kinds! For this challenge, you will work with a partner to develop a slime recipe.

Criteria

For the design to be successful, it must…

- contain a chemical reaction.
- have a non-sticky, slimy consistency.
- have a mix-in that gives it a unique look and/or feel.

Constraints

- The slime recipe may use a maximum of three ingredients (not including mix-ins).
- You may only choose from the ingredients and materials provided to you.

My Summary

_____

_____

_____

_____

My Questions

_____

_____

_____

_____

Name: _____ Date: _____

Directions: Research slime recipes, and answer the questions. Then, brainstorm and record ideas. Discuss ideas with others, and add to your brainstorming.

Day 2

1. What different types of ingredients can be used to make slime?

   _____   _____   _____

   _____   _____   _____

   _____   _____   _____

2. What type of chemical reaction can happen?

   _____

   _____

3. How can slime be different depending on the ingredients?

   _____

   _____

   _____

My Brainstorming

_____

_____

_____

_____

_____

_____

_____

_____

_____

Unit 1: Chemical Reactions

Name: _____ Date: _____

Directions: Write the slime recipe. Include the ingredients, amounts, and steps to make the slime. Sketch what you think your slime will look like. Then, answer the question.

Slime Recipe

_____

_____

_____

_____

_____

_____

_____

1. What concerns do you have about your design?

_____

_____

Name: _____ Date: _____

Directions: Read the questions. Discuss them with your group. Gather your materials. Make your slime. Record notes after you make it.

What will you do if it is too sticky or too watery?

Which team member will add each ingredient?

In what order will you add the ingredients?

Things to Consider

How will you make sure you followed the recipe correctly?

What will you use to mix the ingredients? How long will you mix them?

Slime Making Notes
(surprises, problems, solutions, etc.)

Unit 1: Chemical Reactions

Name: _____ Date: _____

Directions: Evaluate your slime. Then, let a classmate play with your slime, and have them complete their own evaluation.

My Evaluation

Is the slime...	Yes	No
stretchy?		
sticky?		
soft?		
mixed well?		
fun to play with?		

1. How would you rate this slime? A 4 means the slime is amazing, and a 1 means the slime needs work.

   4   3   2   1

2. Explain your answer.

   _____

   _____

Classmate's Evaluation

Is the slime...	Yes	No
stretchy?		
sticky?		
soft?		
mixed well?		
fun to play with?		

3. How would you rate this slime? A 4 means the slime is amazing, and a 1 means the slime needs work.

   4   3   2   1

4. Explain your answer.

   _____

   _____

Name: _____ Date: _____

Directions: Reflect on the evaluation results for your slime. Research and plan how it could be improved.

1. Did your slime turn out the way you planned? Why or why not?

_____

_____

_____

2. What was good about your slime recipe?

_____

_____

_____

3. What could make your slime look, feel, or function better?

_____

_____

_____

The following constraint has been changed:

- The slime may have up to six ingredients, not including the mix-ins.

4. What new ingredients do you want to try?

_____

_____

_____

Name: _____ Date: _____

Directions: Plan and write your new slime recipe. Include the ingredients, amounts, and steps to make the slime. Sketch what you think your slime will look like.

In my redesign, I will...

add _____

remove _____

change _____

New Slime Recipe

_____

_____

_____

_____

_____

_____

Name: _____ Date: _____

Directions: Read the questions. Discuss them with your group. Gather your materials. Remake your slime. Record notes after you make it.

How will you make sure you followed the recipe correctly?

Which team member will add each ingredient?

What will you do if it is too sticky or too watery?

Things to Consider

Will you change the order you add ingredients?

What will you use to mix the ingredients? How long will you mix them?

Slime Remaking Notes
(surprises, problems, solutions, etc.)

Day 4

Name: _____ Date: _____

Directions: Evaluate your slime. Then, let a classmate play with your slime, and have them complete their own evaluation.

My Evaluation

Is the slime...	Yes	No
stretchy?		
sticky?		
soft?		
mixed well?		
fun to play with?		

1. How would you rate this slime? A 4 means the slime is amazing, and a 1 means the slime needs work.

    4   3   2   1

2. Explain your answer.

    _____

    _____

Classmate's Evaluation

Is the slime...	Yes	No
stretchy?		
sticky?		
soft?		
mixed well?		
fun to play with?		

3. How would you rate this slime? A 4 means the slime is amazing, and a 1 means the slime needs work.

    4   3   2   1

4. Explain your answer.

    _____

    _____

Name: _____ Date: _____

Directions: Answer the questions to reflect on your slime.

1. How did this challenge use chemical reactions?

   _____

   _____

   _____

2. Which slime do you think was better? Explain your answer.

   _____

   _____

3. What was most challenging about making slime?

   _____

   _____

   _____

   _____

4. What did you enjoy most in this challenge?

   _____

   _____

5. What advice would you give to someone who wants to make their own slime?

   _____

   _____

   _____

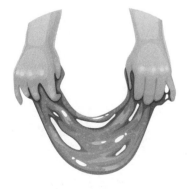

Gravity Teaching Support

Overview of Unit Activities

Students will learn about and explore gravity on Earth through the following activities:

- reading about gravity
- studying a graphic about a hot-air balloon
- experimenting with the drop times of flat and crumpled paper
- making comics about doing daily tasks with little or no gravity
- using a table to explore how gravity affects weight in space
- creating devices that increase the amount of time objects take to reach the ground

Materials Per Group

Week 1

- basic school supplies

STEAM Challenge

- basic school supplies
- books or online resources about helicopter seeds, animals, and parachutes
- calculator
- coffee filters (2)
- fabric (various types)

- plastic wrap
- small box or another object weighing about 1 oz. (30 g)
- stopwatch
- string/yarn (3–4 feet, 1 m)

Setup and Instructional Tips

- Students might request a variety of materials not listed to create their gravity-defying devices. Provide them with their requests at your discretion.
- **Testing Days:** Choose objects for students to drop that weigh about one ounce. Make sure you have enough for each group to receive an identical object. It will be best if the object has a small surface area (to reduce air resistance).
- **STEAM Challenge:** The challenge can be done individually or in groups. Students working in groups should sketch their own designs first. Then, have them share designs in groups and choose one together.

Discussion Questions

- What is gravity?
- What would happen on Earth if there was no gravity? If there was more or less gravity?
- Can gravity be manipulated? How?
- How have humans engineered ways to reduce or slow the effects of gravity?

Additional Notes

- **Possible Misconception:** Heavier objects fall faster than lighter ones.
  Truth: Mass/weight does not affect the speed an object falls; however, greater air resistance can reduce the speed an object falls to the ground.

Scaffolding and Extension Suggestions

- Show students examples of "helicopter" seeds falling, squirrels jumping from heights, and birds flying; facilitate a discussion about the strategies these things use.
- Encourage students to research how companies want to use drones to deliver packages, and challenge students to use those ideas to create their devices.

Answer Key

Week 1 Day 1
1. B
2. A
3. D
4. C

Week 1 Day 2
1. The air has to be hot so it is less dense than the cold air and will rise.
2. Wicker is lightweight and strong.
3. 1783

Week 1 Day 5
1. They would have the lowest weight on the moon.
2. I would not be bigger because my mass would not change. My weight would be more because there is more gravity.
3. The larger the object, the more gravity it has.

Weeks 2 & 3
See STEAM Challenge Rubric on page 221.

Day 1

Name: _____ **Date:** _____

Directions: Read the text, and choose the best answer for each question.

Gravity

Imagine a person waking up in their bed. They walk into the kitchen. They get a cup out of the cabinet and pour orange juice into it. Nothing about that seems remarkable. But it is only possible because of gravity. Gravity is a force that pulls objects toward Earth. Without gravity, that person would be floating down the hallway and chasing down drops of orange juice in the air. People measure how much gravity is pulling on something by its weight. Earth's gravity does not just keep people and objects on the ground. It also pulls on the moon! The moon orbits Earth because of Earth's gravity.

1. Gravity is _____.

  (A) floating
  (B) a force
  (C) an object
  (D) a push

2. What does gravity do?

  (A) pulls objects to Earth
  (B) pushes objects to Earth
  (C) helps objects fall slowly
  (D) keeps objects in the air

3. _____ measures how much gravity is acting on an object.

  (A) Mass
  (B) Force
  (C) Pulling
  (D) Weight

4. Which of these statements is true?

  (A) The moon's gravity pulls on Earth.
  (B) The moon's gravity keeps objects on Earth from floating.
  (C) Earth's gravity pulls on the moon.
  (D) Earth's gravity does not affect the moon.

Name: _____ **Date:** _____

Directions: Read the text, and study the diagram. Then, answer the questions.

Hot-Air Balloons

Gravity might keep people on the ground, but that has never stopped them from dreaming of being up in the clouds! Long before airplanes defied gravity, there were hot-air balloons. In fact, people went up in a hot-air balloon for the first time in 1783.

Hot-air balloons stay afloat because they are filled with hot air. Cold air molecules are closer together, and hot air molecules are farther apart. So, the hot air is less dense and will rise above the cold air. Study the diagram to see the parts of a hot-air balloon.

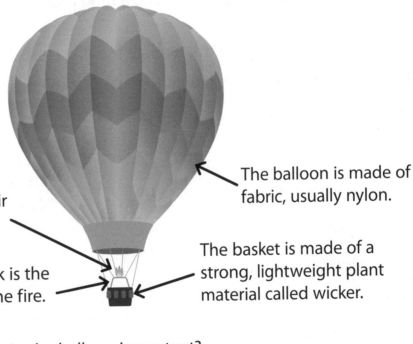

The balloon is made of fabric, usually nylon.

The fire heats the air inside the balloon.

The propane tank is the heat source for the fire.

The basket is made of a strong, lightweight plant material called wicker.

1. Why is heating the air in the balloon important?

_____

_____

2. Why is the basket made of wicker?

_____

_____

3. When did people first travel in a hot-air balloon? _____

Unit 2: Gravity

Name: _____ Date: _____

Directions: Follow the steps to experiment with how different shapes fall.

Question: How can the shape of paper affect how quickly gravity pulls it to the ground?

Materials

paper   stopwatch

Steps

1. Stand from a height (on a ladder, staircase, balcony, etc.). Drop a flat sheet of paper. Use a stopwatch to time how long it takes to reach the ground. Record your results.

2. Fold the paper into fourths. Repeat the drop test. Record your results.

3. Crumple the paper into a tight ball. Repeat the drop test. Record your results.

4. Form a sheet of paper into a shape of your choice. Repeat the drop test. Record your results.

Shape of Paper	Time	Observations of Paper Movement During Drop
flat sheet of paper		
paper folded into fourths		
paper crumpled into ball		
shape of your choice _____		

Talk About It!

Which paper fell in the least amount of time? Why?

What affected the time it took the paper to reach the ground for each drop?

Do you think you could decrease the time it takes the paper to reach the ground? Could you increase it? How?

Name: _____ **Date:** _____

Directions: Imagine a day without gravity! What would eating breakfast be like? Or playing outside at recess? Or doing your homework? Make a comic of yourself trying to do something ordinary without gravity. Add captions, thought bubbles, and speech bubbles.

Name: _____ Date: _____

Directions: Read the text, and study the chart. Then, answer the questions.

People have both mass and weight. Their mass is the amount of matter they are made of, and their weight measures how much gravity is pulling on them. Gravity is the same all over Earth, but it can be different on places in space. Imagine a person traveling all over space. Their mass wouldn't change—they would stay the same size. But their weight would change depending on the amount of gravity.

Location	Weight
Earth	100 pounds (45 kg)
Jupiter	253 pounds (115 kg)
Mercury	38 pounds (17 kg)
Earth's moon	17 pounds (8 kg)
the sun	2,707 pounds (1,228 kg)

1. According to the chart, where would a person weigh the least?

   _____

2. If you weighed 253 pounds (115 kg) on Jupiter, would you be bigger than you are on Earth? Explain your answer.

   _____

   _____

3. Think about the size of the moon and the sun. What inference can you make about gravity and size?

   _____

   _____

   _____

Name: _____ Date: _____

Directions: Read the text. Then, summarize the challenge in your own words. Write any questions you have.

The Challenge

Plants, animals, and people have all found ways to cheat gravity. Gravity cannot be changed. But there are reasons people want to slow down falling objects. For example, some companies want to use drones to deliver packages. But fast-falling packages from the sky are not safe. Imagine you worked for one of these companies. Your challenge is to create a device that slows down a package as it falls. You will drop the object and device from a height and compare its drop time to a control.

Criteria

For the design to be successful, it must…

- slow the speed at which a package falls to the ground (compared to a control).
- clearly show a design for the company (you may create the name or symbol).

Constraints

- You may only use the materials provided to you.
- No electronics may be used.

Testing Note

The package size and weight and the drop height should be the same for all groups.

My Summary

_____

_____

_____

My Questions

_____

_____

_____

Name: _____ Date: _____

Directions: Research how different things fall or drop and answer the questions. Then, brainstorm and record ideas for your device. Discuss ideas with others, and add to your brainstorming.

1. What types of seeds fall slowly to the ground? How do they do it?

   _____

   _____

2. What animals are able to slow down a fall to the ground? How do they do it?

   _____

   _____

   _____

3. How can people slow down a fall from the sky?

   _____

   _____

My Brainstorming

_____

_____

_____

_____

_____

_____

_____

_____

_____

_____

Name: _____ **Date:** _____

Directions: Sketch one or more designs for your package delivery design. Add the symbol or design for the delivery company. List the materials. Then, answer the question.

Materials

_____   _____   _____

_____   _____   _____

1. What concerns do you have about your design?

_____

_____

Unit 2: Gravity

Name: _____ Date: _____

Directions: Gather your materials, plan your steps, and build your delivery device design. Record notes as you build. Then, answer the question.

Delivery Device Building Plan

	Job or Task	Group Member(s)
1		
2		
3		
4		
5		
6		

Building Notes
(additional steps, problems, changes, etc.)

1. What do you think will happen when you test your design?

_____

_____

Name: _____ Date: _____

Directions: Decide as a group what height to test your package delivery devices from. Drop the package without your design for the control. Then, drop the package with your design. For each drop, have two people time how long it takes to reach the ground. Record the times and find their average. Then, answer the questions.

Drop Height: _____

	Timer 1	**Timer 2**	**Average Time**
control			
package with your device			

Note: To find the average, add the two times together and then divide by two.

1. Which drop took longer? _____

2. What was the difference in time? _____

3. Would you consider your design a success? What is your evidence and reasoning?

_____

_____

_____

_____

Name: _____ Date: _____

Directions: Reflect on your design, and answer the questions. Then, plan how you will improve it. Conduct additional research if needed.

1. What went well with your delivery device?

   _____

   _____

   _____

2. What flaws did you discover from testing?

   _____

   _____

   _____

3. How could you make your delivery device work better?

   _____

   _____

   _____

Draw a star next to one or more ways you will improve your design.

- My first design did not meet all the criteria. To improve it, I will

   _____

   _____

- Increase the drop time of your package.
- Drop a delicate item, such as an egg, and keep it from breaking.
- My own idea: _____

   _____

Name: _____ **Date:** _____

Directions: Plan and sketch your new delivery device design. Label the parts and the materials you will use for each part. Then, complete the sentence.

In my redesign, I will…

add _____

remove _____

change _____

1. The change or improvement I am most excited about is _____

_____

_____

Name: _____ Date: _____

Directions: Gather your materials, plan your steps, and rebuild your delivery device design. Record notes as you build. Then, answer the question.

Delivery Device Rebuilding Plan

	Job or Task	Group Member(s)
1		
2		
3		
4		
5		
6		

Building Notes
(surprises, problems, changes, etc.)

Name: _____ **Date:** _____

Directions: Decide as a group what height to test your package delivery devices from. Drop the package without the device for the control. Then, drop the package with the device. For each drop, have two people time how long it takes to reach the ground. Record the times, and find their average. Then, answer the questions.

Drop Height: _____

	Timer 1	**Timer 2**	**Average Time**
control			
package with device			

Note: To find the average, add the two times together and then divide by two.

1. Which drop took longer? _____

2. What was the difference in time? _____

3. Did your new design work better? What is your evidence and reasoning?

_____

_____

_____

_____

Unit 2: Gravity

Name: _____ Date: _____

Directions: Reflect on the work you did for this challenge, and answer the questions.

1. What science concepts did you apply in this challenge?

   _____

   _____

2. How would this challenge have been different if you had dropped a heavier object?

   _____

   _____

3. Do you think drones delivering packages is safe? Explain your answer.

   _____

   _____

4. Draw your delivering device being used in the real world. Write a caption telling what is happening.

Mixtures and Solutions Teaching Support

Overview of Unit Activities

Students will learn about and explore physical changes through the following activities:

- reading about physical changes
- studying graphics about mixtures and solutions
- dissolving salt in water at different temperatures
- creating art by mixing colors of paint
- analyzing a chart showing mixtures and weights of substances
- designing recipes for tasty lemonade

Materials Per Group

Week 1

- bowls (3)
- heat source (kettle, hot plate, etc.; for heating water)
- ice ($\frac{1}{2}$ cup, 125 mL)
- paint (three colors)
- paintbrush
- salt (3 tbsp., 53 g)
- spoon
- water (3–4 cups, 750 mL to 1 L)

STEAM Challenge

- basic school supplies
- cane sugar (1–2 cups, 200–400 g)
- cups (enough for each student to taste test)
- ice (1–2 cups, 250–500 mL)
- lemon extract (2–3 tbsp., 30–45 mL)
- lemon juice (1–2 cups, 250–500 mL)
- lemons (3–4)
- measuring spoons and cups
- online resources or cookbooks with lemonade recipes
- other sugar options (honey, maple syrup, brown sugar; optional)
- pitcher (quart-sized or with 1 quart line marked)
- stopwatch
- toothpicks (2–4; for garnishes)
- various lemonade ingredients/flavorings (strawberries, limes, mint, etc.)

Setup and Instructional Tips

- **Week 1 Day 3:** Use caution when heating water, and only let adults pour or handle hot water.
- **Building Days:** If students are using whole lemons to make juice, they may need help cutting them. Plastic knives can be used with some effort.
- **Testing Days:** Before testing, brainstorm with students the best way to set up the blind taste test.

Discussion Questions

- What are examples of physical properties?
- What changes can happen to water?
- What types of mixtures can you think of?
- How could you separate items in a mixture?
- How do we use solutions and mixtures in our daily lives?
- How does designing a recipe compare with designing a building?

Additional Notes

- **Possible Misconception:** Mixtures cannot be separated.
  Truth: Most mixtures can be undone, some as easily as sorting items in trail mix.

- **Possible Misconception:** Baking is a physical change.
  Truth: Baking is a chemical change because the heat reacts with substances to create new ones.

- **Possible Design Solutions:** Students might try a recipe of equal parts water, sugar, and lemon juice. Students will likely determine this combination needs more water. They might try to add different ingredients, depending on what is available.

Scaffolding and Extension Suggestions

- Give students visual examples of different types of physical changes, including mixtures and solutions. Have them keep track of mixtures and solutions they come across in a day.

- Encourage students to experiment with flavors during week 3. You may choose to allow them to bring approved ingredients from home.

- Encourage students to investigate how more complex mixtures could be separated back into their original substances (paint, beverages).

Answer Key

Week 1 Day 1
1. C
2. D
3. B
4. B

Week 1 Day 2
1. They are physical changes because they do not create new substances.
2. A solution has one substance dissolved into another.
3. Examples: mixtures—vegetable soup, sand and salt, basket of toys; solutions—tomato sauce, soda, glass cleaner

Week 1 Day 5
1. Physical changes do not have any effect on the weight of substances.
2. 105 grams
3. The paper would weigh the same. Ripping is a physical change and that does not make a change in weight.

Weeks 2 & 3
See STEAM Challenge Rubric on page 221.

Name: _____ **Date:** _____

Directions: Read the text, and choose the best answer for each question.

Physical Changes

Change is happening all the time. There are different ways things can change. Substances like cloth, water, and paper can go through physical changes. This means their physical properties can change. A cloth might be cut into pieces. Water might freeze into ice. Paper might be crumpled up into a ball. The size, shape, or state of matter were changed, but nothing new was created—the water, cloth, and paper are still those same things. Many physical changes can be undone. They are not permanent. The cloth can be sewn back together, the ice can melt back into water, and the paper can be smoothed out.

substance—a particular kind of material, or matter

1. What is an example of a physical change?

   (A) changing one substance into a different one

   (B) changing a substance using heat

   (C) changing the size or shape of a substance

   (D) changing the way a substance is used

2. Which of these statements is true?

   (A) Physical changes create odors.

   (B) Physical changes create new substances.

   (C) Physical changes need heat.

   (D) Physical changes can often be undone.

3. Water freezing is an example of what type of physical change?

   (A) changing size

   (B) changing state of matter

   (C) changing shape

   (D) changing color

4. What is another example of a physical change?

   (A) Wood burns into ash.

   (B) A soda can is crumpled.

   (C) A firework explodes.

   (D) Batter is cooked into pancakes.

Unit 3: Mixtures and Solutions

Name: _____ Date: _____

Directions: Read the text, and study the pictures. Then, answer the questions.

dissolve—to mix with a liquid and become part of it

Mixtures and Solutions

Mixture	**Solution**
a combination of two or more substances that are not chemically combined	a special type of mixture where a substance is dissolved into a liquid substance

1. Why are the creations of mixtures and solutions considered physical changes?

   _____

   _____

2. How is a solution different from a mixture?

   _____

   _____

3. Give an example of each.

   mixture: _____

   solution: _____

Name: _____ **Date:** _____

Directions: Follow the steps to investigate solutions.

> **Question:** Will salt dissolve faster in water that is hot, cold, or room temperature?
>
> My prediction: _____
>
> _____

Materials

3 bowls	2 cups	heat source	ice
salt	spoon	stopwatch	water

Steps

1. Prepare cold water—add ice and water into a cup. Prepare hot water—have an adult begin heating some water. Prepare room temperature water—place a cup of water on a surface in the room for a few minutes.

2. Put one spoonful of salt in each bowl.

3. Add room temperature water to one bowl and stir. Time how long it takes for the salt to dissolve.

4. Add ice water (but no ice) to the second bowl and stir. Time how long it takes for the salt to dissolve.

5. Have an adult add hot water to the third bowl and stir. Time how long it takes for the salt to dissolve.

Water Temperature	Time to Dissolve (No Visible Salt Left)
room	
cold	
hot	

Talk About It!

Which water temperature dissolved the salt faster? How could this information be helpful when cooking? How could you separate the salt from the water after it has been dissolved?

Unit 3: Mixtures and Solutions

Name: _____ Date: _____

Directions: Mixing paint is an artistic way to show physical changes. Paint a picture using only three colors of paint. Mix the colors to create many shades in your artwork.

What colors will you use? List them.

_____ _____ _____

Name: _____ Date: _____

Directions: Study the table. Then, answer the questions.

	Substance 1	Substance 2	Total Weight When Mixed
Mixture 1	red chocolate candies—1 ounce (30 grams)	green chocolate candies—1 ounce (30 grams)	2 ounces (60 grams)
Mixture 2	grass seed—2 pounds (0.9 kg)	soil—10 pounds (4.5 kg)	12 pounds (5.4 kg)
Mixture 3	yellow paint—12 grams (0.4 ounces)	red paint—15 grams (0.5 ounces)	27 grams (0.9 ounces)

1. What conclusion can you make about how physical changes affect the weight of substances?

   _____

   _____

2. If 30 grams of sawdust, 25 grams of dirt, and 50 grams of sand were mixed, what would the mixture's weight be?

   _____

   _____

3. What would happen to the weight of a sheet of paper that was ripped in half? Explain your answer.

   _____

   _____

Name: _____ Date: _____

Directions: Read the text. Then, summarize the challenge in your own words. Write any questions you have.

The Challenge

Lemonade stands are a fun way for kids like you to make some money. Lemonade is a solution made from a few different substances. For this challenge, you will work with a group of classmates to create a delicious solution of homemade lemonade. They say we eat (and drink) with our eyes first. A glass of your lemonade should look appealing. A classroom-wide taste test will decide whose lemonade is best. Will your group win?

Criteria

For the lemonade recipe to be successful, it must

- be a solution.
- taste good to fellow classmates.
- include at least one garnish for a glass of lemonade (edible or inedible).

Constraints

- Make one quart (473 mL) of lemonade.
- Use no more than four ingredients in the solution.
- You may only use the materials and ingredients provided to you.

My Summary

_____

_____

_____

My Questions

_____

_____

_____

Name: _____ Date: _____

Directions: Research lemonade recipes. Then, answer the questions and brainstorm your ideas. Discuss ideas with others, and add to your brainstorming.

1. What different types of lemonade did you discover?

   _____

   _____

2. What ingredients will you need?

   _____

   _____

3. What types of garnishes, edible and inedible, can be added to lemonade?

   _____

   _____

My Brainstorming

_____

_____

_____

_____

_____

_____

_____

 Talk About It!

Do you like drinks that are more sour or sweet?
How might this influence your recipe?

Name: _____ Date: _____

Directions: Plan two possible recipes for your lemonade. Draw a star next to the one you think will taste best. List any other materials you will need. Write any notes you have about your recipe design.

Recipe 1

Ingredients	Amount

Recipe 2

Ingredients	Amount

Other Materials

_____ _____

_____ _____

Notes

Name: _____ Date: _____

Directions: Read the questions. Discuss them with your group. Then, make your lemonade. Record notes as or after you make it.

Which team member will add each ingredient?

How will you make sure everything is dissolved?

Things to Consider

How will you make sure you followed the recipe correctly?

In what order should you add the ingredients?

Notes
(surprises, challenges, observations)

_____

_____

_____

_____

Name: _____ Date: _____

Directions: Set up a blind taste test for your group's lemonade samples. Complete the table as you taste the samples from other groups. Rank the samples from your favorite to your least favorite. Take a class poll. Share your notes with the other groups. Discuss what you did or did not like about their recipes.

Lemonade Sample	My Thoughts

1. My ranking of the lemonade samples:

_____ _____ _____ _____ _____
(favorite)   (least favorite)

2. My group's lemonade ranked _____.

Name: _____ Date: _____

Directions: Reflect on the taste test results for your lemonade. Research and plan how it could be improved.

1. Was your lemonade too sweet?   yes   no

2. Was your lemonade too sour?   yes   no

3. Was your lemonade too watery?   yes   no

4. What other feedback did you get about your lemonade during the taste test?

_____

_____

5. What ideas did you get from trying other lemonade recipes?

_____

_____

Redesign Time

You will have the opportunity to redesign your lemonade recipe. The following constraint has been changed:

- You may use up to *six* different ingredients.

6. What changes are you thinking of making to improve your recipe?

_____

_____

_____

Unit 3: Mixtures and Solutions

Name: _____ Date: _____

Directions: Plan two new recipes for your lemonade. Draw a star next to the one you think will taste best. List any other materials you will need. Then, complete the sentence.

New Recipe 1

Ingredients	Amount

New Recipe 2

Ingredients	Amount

Other Materials

_____ _____

_____ _____

1. This recipe will taste better because _____

_____

_____

_____

Name: _____ Date: _____

Directions: Discuss the questions with your group. Then, follow your new recipe to make your lemonade. Record notes as or after you make it.

Which team member will add each ingredient?

How will you make sure everything is dissolved?

Things to Consider

What changes do you need to make for the new recipe?

Should the order you combine the ingredients change or stay the same?

Notes
(surprises, challenges, observations)

_____

_____

_____

_____

_____

Name: _____ Date: _____

Directions: Set up a blind taste test for your group's lemonade samples. Complete the table as you taste the samples from other groups. Rank the samples from your favorite to your least favorite, and take a class vote. Share your notes with the other groups. Discuss improvements you noticed to the tastes of the different lemonades.

Lemonade Sample	My Thoughts

1. My ranking of the lemonade samples:

_____ _____ _____ _____ _____

(favorite)   (least favorite)

2. My group's lemonade ranked _____.

Day 5

Name: _____ **Date:** _____

Directions: Reflect on the work you did for this challenge. Answer the questions.

1. How did your group's rankings compare on the first and second tests?

   _____

   _____

2. Which lemonade(s) did you find the most visually appealing? Why?

   _____

   _____

3. What advice would you give to kids who want to start a lemonade stand?

   _____

   _____

   _____

4. Draw yourself working during this challenge. Write a caption telling what you are doing.

   ┌───┐
   │   │
   │   │
   │   │
   │   │
   │   │
   └───┘

 **Try This!**

Set up a lemonade stand in your school or neighborhood. Raise money for a cause you are passionate about.

Properties of Matter Teaching Support

Overview of Unit Activities

Students will learn about and explore properties of matter through the following activities:

- reading about physical properties
- studying graphics about ways to classify matter
- going on scavenger hunts for items with different physical properties
- drawing molecules for different states of matter
- analyzing a table showing density of different objects
- insulating ice cubes to prevent them from melting

Materials Per Group

Week 1

- basic school supplies
- cup of water
- magnet
- ruler
- scale

STEAM Challenge

- basic school supplies
- bubble wrap
- cotton balls (20–30)
- foam
- foil
- graduated cylinder
- heat source (lamp, heater, sun, etc.)
- ice (1 small bowl)
- packaging materials
- shoebox with lid
- small bowl or cup
- scale
- thermometers (2)

Setup and Instructional Tips

- **Week 1 Day 3:** Students will need to test to find objects that sink and float. Ask them to show you which objects they want to test for your approval.

- **STEAM Challenge:** The challenge can be done individually or in groups. Students working in groups should sketch their own designs first. Then, have them share designs in groups and choose one together.

- **Materials:** Students might request a variety of materials not listed to create their insulation. Provide them with their requests when possible.

Discussion Questions

- How can you tell what something is or what it is made of?
- What is a physical property?
- What types of questions might you ask to learn about an unknown substance?
- Why would scientists need to tell substances apart?

Additional Notes

- **Possible Misconception:** Steam is hot air.
  Truth: Steam is water vapor.
- **Potential Design Solution:** Students may place the ice in the center of the box and line it with different materials, such as cotton balls and aluminum foil.

Scaffolding and Extension Suggestions

- Brainstorm several examples of testable, observable, and measurable ways of gathering data with students.
- Challenge students to learn more about thermal energy and how it can be maintained or shared in real-world applications.

Answer Key

Week 1 Day 1
1. D
2. A
3. D
4. C

Week 1 Day 2
1. measurable
2. I could look to see what color the fabric is. I could also observe the texture, shape, and size.
3. Will the egg float in water?

Week 1 Day 5
1. baking soda
2. powdered sugar and cornstarch
3. This is measurable because the substances were weighed, and the data is numbers.

Weeks 2 & 3
See STEAM Challenge Rubric on page 221.

Name: _____ Date: _____

Directions: Read the text, and choose the best answer for each question.

Physical Properties

With so many substances in the world, it is no wonder scientists need ways to identify them. Sometimes, it is easy. If salt and pepper are mixed together, most people could tell them apart by looking. But what if salt and sugar were mixed?

Physical properties can be used to learn about materials. This means learning something about the material that can be measured or tested. Color is a physical property, like the salt and pepper. But there are many more properties that can be examined. For example, is it hard or soft? Is it magnetic? How dense is it? Does it sink or float? Can it conduct heat or electricity? At what temperature does it melt or freeze? Scientists can test these different physical properties. Then, they can figure out what a substance is. Salt and sugar taste different, but they also have different melting points. If you heated them both in a pan, sugar would melt first.

1. A physical property is something that can be _____.

   (A) measured

   (B) tested

   (C) observed

   (D) all of the above

2. Which of these is *not* a physical property of a person?

   (A) emotion

   (B) height

   (C) eye color

   (D) weight

3. If you wanted to identify a type of metal, which physical property would be best to test?

   (A) color

   (B) shape

   (C) size

   (D) magnetism

4. If you wanted to identify salt from sugar without tasting them, which physical property could you test?

   (A) magnetism

   (B) density

   (C) melting point

   (D) color

Name: _____ **Date:** _____

Directions: Read the text, and study the table. Then, answer the questions.

Classifying Matter

Classifying means putting things into groups. The groups are based on certain qualities. For example, music could be classified as country, jazz, or pop. Scientists can classify substances. They use physical properties to help. The properties can be measurable, testable, or observable.

measurable—data able to be expressed in numbers	**testable**—able to be proven true or false when using the scientific method	**observable**—capable of being seen or noticed
	Did it attract a magnet? ☐ yes ☐ no	

1. If you were going to weigh an object, what type of property would that be?

   _____

2. Imagine you were trying to classify a type of fabric. What type of observable data could you find and describe?

   _____

   _____

3. If an object sinks in water, it is more dense than water. If it floats, it is less dense. What is a testable question you could ask about the density of an egg?

   _____

   _____

Unit 4: Properties of Matter

Name: _____ Date: _____

Directions: Go on a scavenger hunt. Write or draw each object or substance in the box.

Tools for Testing and Measuring
magnet   glass of water   ruler   scale

Properties of Matter Scavenger Hunt

something magnetic	something liquid	something smaller than 3 cm
something that floats	something that sinks	something bumpy
something that weighs close to 1 pound	something purple	something that feels cold

Name: _____ **Date:** _____

Directions: Read the text. Fill each star with smaller stars that show the molecules as a solid, liquid, and gas.

The three states of matter are properties that can help a substance be classified. In a solid, such as ice, the molecules are packed very tightly together. They cannot move much at all. If ice is heated enough, it melts into a liquid. The molecules are farther apart and can move more. If water is heated enough, it changes to a gas. The molecules are far apart and can move all over the place!

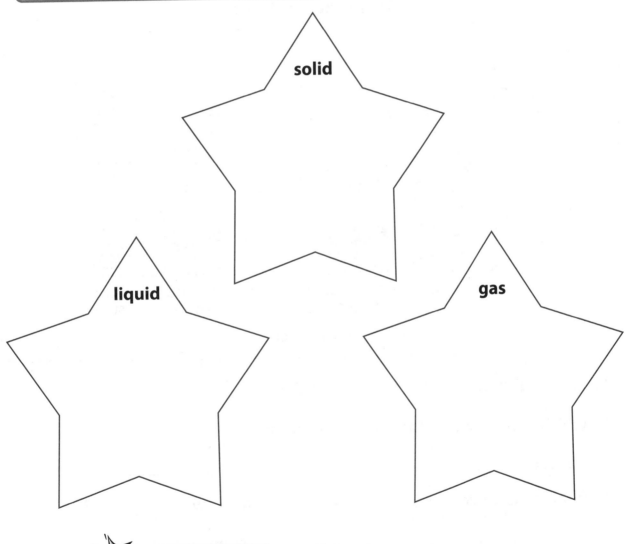

 Try This!

Work with a group to act out how molecules look and move in ice, water, and water vapor.

Day 5

Name: _____ Date: _____

Directions: Read about density. Then, study the bar graph, and answer the questions.

Density is a property of matter. Density is the amount of matter in something. It is shown by the relationship between its weight and size. This means two things might be the same size or have the same amount, but they do not have the same weight. Imagine one tablespoon of salt and one of sugar. The salt weighs 15 grams (0.53 ounces). The same amount of sugar weighs 13 grams (0.46 ounces). The salt has more density.

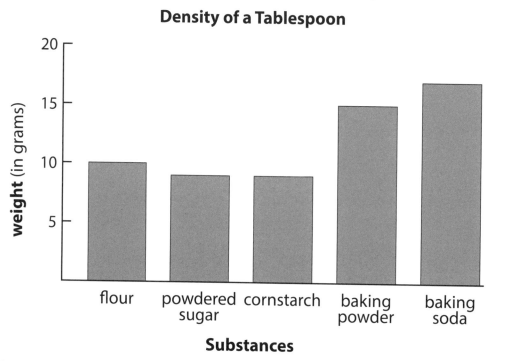

Density of a Tablespoon

weight (in grams) — 20, 15, 10, 5

flour · powdered sugar · cornstarch · baking powder · baking soda

Substances

1. Which substance has the greatest density? _____

2. Which two substances have the same density?

_____

3. Is this observable, measurable, or testable data? How do you know?

_____

_____

Name: _____ **Date:** _____

Directions: Read the text. Then, summarize the challenge in your own words. Write any questions you have.

The Challenge

People use ice for many reasons. It can keep a drink cold or prevent an injury from swelling. But as soon as an ice cube is taken out of freezing temperatures, it begins to change. Without insulation, the ice begins to melt. Summer is approaching, and people are headed outdoors. They want a way to keep their drinks cold. You must design a portable cooler to keep ice frozen. For this challenge, you will insulate an ice cube to keep it from melting.

Criteria

For the cooler design to be successful, it must…

- insulate a bowl of ice and keep it from melting.
- be easily portable.

Constraint

- You may only use the materials provided to you.

My Summary

_____

_____

_____

_____

My Questions

_____

_____

_____

_____

Name: _____ Date: _____

Directions: Research insulation and ways to keep ice from melting too quickly. Answer the questions. Then, brainstorm and record ideas for your cooler design. Discuss ideas with others, and add to your brainstorming.

1. What types of materials are known for being good insulators?

   _____

2. How can coolers and insulated cups keep ice from melting?

   _____

   _____

3. What are some shapes and designs of portable coolers that you like? Draw one or more examples.

   [ ]

   My Brainstorming

   _____

   _____

   _____

   _____

   _____

Name: _____ Date: _____

Directions: Sketch one or more designs for your portable cooler. Show where the ice will go, and list the materials. Then, answer the question.

Materials

_____   _____   _____

_____   _____   _____

1. What concerns do you have about your design?

_____

_____

Unit 4: Properties of Matter

Name: _____ **Date:** _____

Directions: Gather your materials, plan your steps, and build your portable cooler device. Record notes as you build.

Portable Cooler Building Plan

	Job or Task	Group Member(s)
1		
2		
3		
4		
5		
6		

Building Notes
(additional steps, problems, changes to the design, etc.)

Quick Tip!

During building, add the bowl that will hold the ice in your cooler, but don't add the ice yet!

© Shell Education

Name: _____ Date: _____

Directions: Follow the steps to test your cooler.

1. Fill the small bowl in your cooler with ice, and record the number of pieces of ice.

2. Place a thermometer inside the cooler and close the lid.

3. Place a thermometer next to your cooler.

4. Place your cooler under a heat source for 10 minutes.

5. Open the lid and record the new temperatures. Remove the bowl of ice. Pour any water into a graduated cylinder, and record the results.

Number of Ice Cubes: _____

	Inside the Cooler	Outside the Cooler	Change
Starting Temperature			
Ending Temperature			

Amount of Melted Ice: _____

Unit 4: Properties of Matter

Name: _____ Date: _____

Directions: Reflect on your design, and answer the questions. Then, plan how you will improve it. Conduct additional research if needed.

1. Compare the designs and results of others. What parts or materials seemed to work best to keep the ice frozen?

   _____

   _____

   _____

2. What could make the cooler design work better?

   _____

   _____

   _____

Draw a star next to one or more ways you will improve your design.

- My first design did not meet all the criteria. To improve it, I will

  _____

  _____

- Test the cooler for a longer amount of time.
- Reduce the final temperature inside the cooler and the amount of ice that melts.
- My own idea: _____

  _____

Name: _____ Date: _____

Directions: Plan and sketch your new portable cooler design. Label the parts and the materials you will use for each part.

In my redesign, I will…

add _____

remove _____

change _____

1. The change or improvement I think will make the biggest difference is

_____

_____

Day 3

Name: _____ Date: _____

Directions: Build your redesigned cooler. Draw or write about your new plan.

Materials

_____   _____

_____   _____

Name: _____ **Date:** _____

Directions: Follow the steps to test your cooler.

1. Fill the small bowl in your cooler with ice. Use the same number of ice cubes as the first test.

2. Place a thermometer inside the cooler and close the lid.

3. Place a thermometer next to your cooler.

4. Place your cooler under a heat source for 10 minutes (or longer if you choose).

5. Open the lid, and record the new temperatures. Remove the bowl of ice. Pour any water into a graduated cylinder and record the results.

Number of Ice Cubes: _____

	Inside the Cooler	**Outside the Cooler**	**Change**
Starting Temperature			
Ending Temperature			

Amount of Melted Ice: _____

Name: _____ Date: _____

Directions: Reflect on the work you did for this challenge. Answer the questions.

1. Do you think your first or second test was more successful? What is your evidence and reasoning?

   _____

   _____

   _____

2. Why is knowing how to insulate something to keep it cold a good skill?

   _____

   _____

3. How was the insulation in your cooler different from something you might find in a store? How was it the same?

   _____

   _____

   _____

4. Draw a picture of yourself doing something you enjoyed. Write a caption.	5. Draw a picture of yourself solving a problem. Write a caption.

Bones and Skeletons Teaching Support

Overview of Unit Activities

Students will learn about and explore bones and skeletons through the following activities:

- reading about bones
- reading about vertebrates and invertebrates
- experimenting with how humans bend their bodies
- creating human skeletons from cotton swabs
- examining a diagram of a bird's skeleton
- building articulated model hands

Materials Per Group

Week 1

- basic school supplies
- cotton swabs (both whole and cut into different lengths)
- pipe cleaners (3)
- straws (3)

STEAM Challenge

- basic school supplies
- books or online resources about robotics and model hands
- books or online resources with the American Sign Language (ASL) alphabet
- cardboard sheets (2–3)
- cardstock
- craft sticks (5–10)
- disposable gloves (2)
- fishing line (3–4 feet, 1 m)
- modeling clay
- pipe cleaners (10–15)
- straws (10–15)
- wire (different gauges; optional)
- yarn (3–4 feet, 1 m)

Setup and Instructional Tips

- **STEAM Challenge:** The challenge can be done individually or in groups. Students working in groups should sketch their own designs first. Then, have them share designs in groups and choose one together.

Discussion Questions

- Why do people have bones?
- What might happen if a person did not have some bones?
- Do all animals have bones? How do you know?
- How do bones differ from one animal to the next?
- How have engineers modeled the functions of bones and joints in other machines and tools?

Additional Notes

- **Possible Misconception:** Bones are hard all the way to the center.
  Truth: Human bones are like a sponge in the center and produce blood cells there.

- **Possible Design Solutions:** Students might thread yarn through straw pieces on a hand-shaped piece of cardboard. They might use rolled paper pieces and fit them inside each other to create joints. Pipe cleaners might be used to create bendable fingers. Students might test different materials, such as yarn or wire, to pull the fingers into different positions.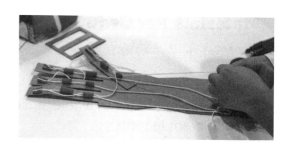

Scaffolding and Extension Suggestions

- Help struggling students plan their model hands by showing them examples and giving them time to talk through their ideas.

Answer Key

Week 1 Day 1
1. D
2. B
3. C
4. A

Week 1 Day 2
1. Vertebrates have bones inside their bodies and invertebrates do not.
2. A disadvantage for an invertebrate is that their bodies are not as strong or able to withstand attack.
3. An exoskeleton is a hard outer covering an invertebrate might have.

Week 1 Day 5
1. The wing bones are very long and narrow compared to the full wing covered in feathers.
2. Their knees are high and bend like humans' do. Their ankles are where people's knees are, so it looks like their knees are bending backwards.
3. An advantage of hollow bones is they are light to help birds fly. A disadvantage is they are not very strong and break easily.

Weeks 2 & 3
See STEAM Challenge Rubric on page 221.

Name: _____ Date: _____

Directions: Read the text, and choose the best answer for each question.

Bones

People can stand, sit, or lie down, and their body parts stay the same sizes and shapes. This is because of the bones that make up their skeletons. A person has 206 bones—and about half of them are in the hands and feet! Without their skeleton, a person would flop around and have little ability to move. Bones give a body structure and protect important organs. For example, the ribs protect the fragile lungs and heart. Bones also make blood cells and store minerals, such as calcium. If a person doesn't have enough calcium, their body will take it from the bones. Eating foods high in calcium and exercising help keep bones healthy. The outsides of human bones are very hard, but the insides are like sponges. Bones are strong and do not break easily, but if they do break, they can heal. Wearing a cast keeps the bone straight as it heals.

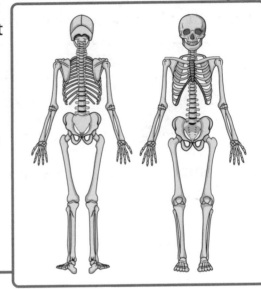

1. The inside of a bone is _____.

(A) impossible to break

(B) like a rock

(C) very hard

(D) like a sponge

2. Which could be the number of bones in the hands and feet?

(A) 63

(B) 106

(C) 220

(D) 12

3. What do bones *not* do?

(A) protect organs

(B) store minerals

(C) make calcium

(D) provide structure

4. Why do doctors put casts on broken bones?

(A) to keep the bone straight

(B) to speed up the bone's healing

(C) to allow the bone time to grow

(D) to help the bone make new blood cells

Unit 5: Bones and Skeletons

Day 2

Name: _____ Date: _____

Directions: Read the text, and study the chart. Then, answer the questions.

Vertebrates and Invertebrates

Bones might seem necessary for all animals, but they are not. In fact, 90% of living creatures do not have skeletons inside their bodies. These animals are called invertebrates. They might have shells like crabs, or hard outer coverings like beetles. These are called exoskeletons. Some creatures might not have any structures to their bodies at all. Think of jellyfish or slugs! Animals with bones inside their bodies are called vertebrates.

Vertebrates		Invertebrates	
amphibian	mammal	spider	worm
reptile	fish	insect	jellyfish
bird		mollusk	

1. What is the difference between vertebrates and invertebrates?

   _____

2. What might be a disadvantage for an invertebrate?

   _____

   _____

3. What is an exoskeleton?

   _____

   _____

Name: _____ **Date:** _____

Directions: Follow the steps to learn about bones.

> **Question:** How can people bend their bodies if bones are so hard?

Materials

pipe cleaners   straws   scissors

Steps

1. Put a pipe cleaner "bone" inside a straw and try to bend it.

2. Cut a straw in half. Put a pipe cleaner through the straw pieces and try to bend it.

3. Cut a straw in half. Then, cut each half of the straw into five pieces. Thread the pieces on a pipe cleaner and try to bend it.

joint—the place where two bones meet to allow movement, such as an elbow, shoulder, or knee

Talk About It!

Which straw was similar to your backbone? To your thigh? To your elbow?

What would happen if your arm were one long bone?

How does the length of the bone affect movement?

What other ways could you model bone movements?

Name: _____ Date: _____

Directions: Create a human skeleton using cotton swabs. The skull and pelvis have been added for you.

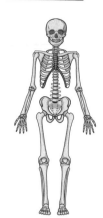

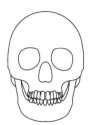

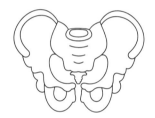

Name: _____ Date: _____

Directions: Study the diagram of a bird skeleton. Then, answer the questions.

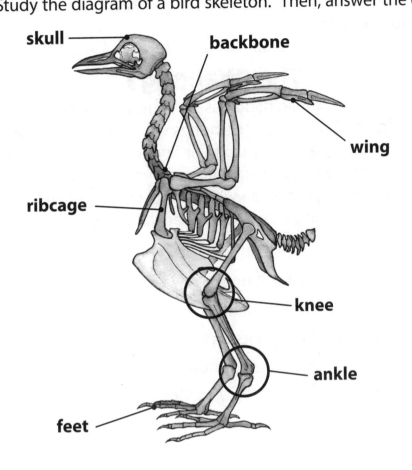

skull

backbone

wing

ribcage

knee

ankle

feet

1. What do you notice about the wing bones?

_____

_____

2. A bird's legs appear to bend backwards, but they do not. Use the skeleton to explain why.

_____

_____

3. Birds' bones are hollow. What advantage could this give birds? What disadvantage?

_____

_____

_____

Day 1

Name: _____ Date: _____

Directions: Read the text. Then, summarize the challenge in your own words. Write any questions you have.

The Challenge

Did you know each human hand has 27 bones? All of these bones give hands their shape and structure. The bones work with muscles and tendons so a person can hold a pencil or snap their fingers. Scientists have made robotic hands, which can help people in many ways. For this challenge, imagine you want to help a person who cannot use their hand. You will create a simple model hand with fingers that can move.

Criteria

For the design to be successful, it must…

- have four fingers and one thumb.
- be fully articulated (have joints on each finger that can be moved).
- be able to make a thumbs-up gesture.
- be able to finger spell a word in American Sign Language (ASL) that is at least four letters long.

Constraint

- You may only use the materials provided to you.

muscle—body tissue that can contract and cause movement

tendon—tissue that connects muscle to bone

My Summary

_____

_____

_____

My Questions

_____

_____

_____

Name: _____ Date: _____

Directions: Research robotic model hands, and answer the questions. Then, brainstorm and record ideas. Discuss ideas with others, and add to your brainstorming.

1. Describe how robotic model hands are used in the world today.

_____

_____

2. Draw two examples of robotic hands you found.

Example 1	Example 2

3. What ideas from these high-tech robotic hands could you apply to your low-tech model hand?

_____

_____

My Brainstorming

_____

_____

_____

_____

_____

Name: _____ Date: _____

Directions: Sketch one or more designs for your model hand design. List the materials. Describe how you will be able to make the fingers move. Then, answer the question.

Materials

_____   _____   _____

_____   _____   _____

How It Will Work

_____

_____

1. What word will you spell in ASL? _____

Name: _____ Date: _____

Directions: Gather your materials, plan your steps, and build your articulated model hand. Record notes as you build.

Model Hand Building Plan

	Job or Task	Group Member(s)
1		
2		
3		
4		
5		
6		

Building Notes
(additional steps, problems, changes, etc.)

 Quick Tip!

It is okay to do a few mini tests as you build! Can you move all four fingers and the thumb?

Can you make the fingers move to spell a word in ASL?

Unit 5: Bones and Skeletons

Name: _____ Date: _____

Directions: Demonstrate your model hand for the class. Complete the chart to evaluate your model. Explain or elaborate on your evaluation in the Notes column.

	Yes	No	Notes
Does the model have four fingers and one thumb?			
Is it fully articulated?			
Can it do a thumbs-up gesture?			
Can it spell a word using ASL? word: _____			

Day 1

Name: _____ Date: _____

Directions: Reflect on your design, and answer the questions. Plan how you will improve it. Conduct additional research if needed.

1. What parts and materials worked well in your model hand design?

   _____

   _____

   _____

2. What could make the model work even better?

   _____

   _____

   _____

The following changes have been made to the criteria for this challenge:

   • The model hand must be able to pick up a writing utensil.

   • The model hand must be able to hold the writing utensil as you move it to write a word that is at least three letters.

3. What changes could you make to help your model hand meet the new criteria?

   _____

   _____

   _____

   _____

Day 2

Name: _____ Date: _____

Directions: Plan and sketch your new model hand design. Label the parts and the materials you will use for each part.

In my redesign, I will...

add _____

remove _____

change _____

1. I think this new design will work better because _____

_____

_____

Name: _____ Date: _____

Directions: Gather your materials, plan your steps, and rebuild your articulated model hand. Record notes as you build.

Model Hand Rebuilding Plan

	Job or Task	Group Member(s)
1		
2		
3		
4		
5		
6		

Building Notes
(additional steps, problems, changes, etc.)

Unit 5: Bones and Skeletons

Name: _____ Date: _____

Directions: Demonstrate your model hand for the class. Have your model hand write a word in the space. Then, complete the chart to evaluate your model.

	Yes	No	Notes
Can the model pick up a writing utensil?			
Can it write a word? word: _____			

Name: _____ **Date:** _____

Directions: Reflect on the work you did for this challenge. Answer the questions.

1. What was challenging about making your model hand?

   _____

   _____

2. What part of your model represented bones? What would have happened during your demonstration if they were not there?

   _____

   _____

3. What changes do you think will be made to hand robotics in the future?

   _____

   _____

4. Draw yourself during a part of this challenge you enjoyed. Write a caption telling what you are doing.

Decomposers Teaching Support

Overview of Unit Activities

Students will learn about and explore decomposers through the following activities:

- reading about decomposers
- studying graphics of different types of decomposers
- beginning experiments about composting
- drawing larger-than-life size illustrations of decomposers
- using a food web diagram to answer questions
- presenting an informative lesson with visual aids about decomposers and food webs

Materials Per Group

Week 1

- basic school supplies
- disposable gloves
- food scraps (vegetable peels, fruit rinds, etc.)

- small plastic tub
- soil
- water

STEAM Challenge

- basic school supplies
- books or online resources about food webs
- construction paper
- images of decomposers

- modeling clay
- poster board
- shoebox
- yarn (3–4 feet, 1 m)

Setup and Instructional Tips

- **Week 1 Day 3:** If possible, keep the compost in the classroom for two weeks so students can continue to observe it.
- **STEAM Challenge:** The challenge can be done individually or in groups. Students working in groups should sketch their own designs first. Then, have them share designs in groups and choose one together.
- If possible, arrange for students to give their presentations to small groups of younger students.

Discussion Questions

- What are the different parts of a food web?
- What happens to dead plants and animals?
- How can nature recycle?
- What are decomposers, and why are they important?

Additional Notes

- **Possible Misconception:** Decomposers can break down anything.
  Truth: Many human-made materials, such as plastic and glass, take hundreds to millions of years to decompose.
- **Possible Design Solutions:** Students may choose to make posters for their visual aids, but encourage them to think beyond that. Offer suggestions such as dioramas, clay models, or slideshow presentations. During Week 3, students might make interactive visual aids by having younger students move clay pieces, connect food web components with yarn, or write on the visual aids.

Scaffolding and Extension Suggestions

- Preview important vocabulary with students. Show them examples of decomposers and discuss how they help soil.
- Challenge students to learn about decomposers in extreme habitats such as the tundra or in the ocean. Encourage them to learn about which materials do not easily decompose.

Answer Key

Week 1 Day 1
1. C
2. C
3. A
4. D

Week 1 Day 2
1. The apple is getting smaller and more shrunken.
2. A decomposer such as a worm, beetle, ant, fungi, or bacteria could have made the change.
3. The apple has been broken down and has become part of the ground.

Week 1 Day 5
1. The mouse gets energy from the grass.
2. Owl droppings are being decomposed.
3. The decomposer puts energy from the owl droppings back into the ground and the producer can use it to grow.

Weeks 2 & 3
See STEAM Challenge Rubric on page 221.

Unit 6: Decomposers

Name: _____ Date: _____

Directions: Read the text, and choose the best answer for each question.

Decomposers

Food webs begin with the sun. It gives energy to plants, and they pass energy to animals. But plants and animals make waste. Leaves and fruit fall to the ground, animals have droppings, and all living things die. So, what happens to all that waste? Bring in the decomposers! These organisms eat this waste and break it down. The nutrients and energy that were in the waste go back into the ground. Earthworms are decomposers, as are some types of beetles and ants. Microscopic bacteria are decomposers. They cannot be seen by the naked eye, but these tiny organisms break down waste. Mold and mildew are forms of fungi, and they are also decomposers. This important part of the food web is sometimes called nature's garbage disposal. Without them, the ground would be covered in waste.

1. Decomposers get energy directly from _____.
   - (A) the sun
   - (B) animals
   - (C) natural waste
   - (D) plants

2. Which is an example of decomposing?
   - (A) A plant creates oxygen.
   - (B) A leaf falls off of a tree.
   - (C) A worm breaks down a dead mouse.
   - (D) A deer eats berries from a bush.

3. Which is *not* an example of a decomposer?
   - (A) an apple
   - (B) bacteria
   - (C) an earthworm
   - (D) mold

4. How is decomposing like recycling?
   - (A) The organisms get energy from the sun.
   - (B) Plants and animals make natural waste.
   - (C) The decomposers break down the waste.
   - (D) Nutrients from the waste are put back into the ground.

Name: _____ Date: _____

Directions: Read the text, and study the pictures. Then, answer the questions.

A Decomposing Apple

Imagine passing by an apple tree. You notice an apple on the ground and decide to check on the apple every few weeks for two months. You see it begin to change. One day, it is gone. Decomposers have done their job.

| Day 1 | Day 20 | Day 40 | Day 60 |

1. Describe the changes you see in the pictures.

_____

_____

_____

_____

2. What could have caused the change in the apple?

_____

_____

_____

3. Where has the apple gone?

_____

_____

_____

Unit 6: Decomposers

Name: _____ Date: _____

Directions: Follow the steps to complete an investigation about composting.

Question: What happens to food waste over time?

Materials

soil   food scraps   water
disposable gloves   small plastic tub

Steps

1. Fill a small plastic tub about halfway with soil.

2. Mix in food scraps.

3. Add a few sprays of water to the mixture. Cover the soil with the lid.

4. Check on the soil every few days for two weeks.

compost—soil mixed with plant and food waste that breaks down and becomes nutrient-rich

Talk About It!

What do you think will happen over time?
What advantages are there to composting?
How does composting relate to decomposition?

Name: _____ **Date:** _____

Directions: There are many different types of decomposers. But they are all small. Find a picture of a decomposer and draw it giant-sized. Be sure to include details people might miss on a life-sized version. Draw other objects next to it to show how big it is.

Day 5

Name: _____ Date: _____

Directions: Study the food web, and answer the questions.

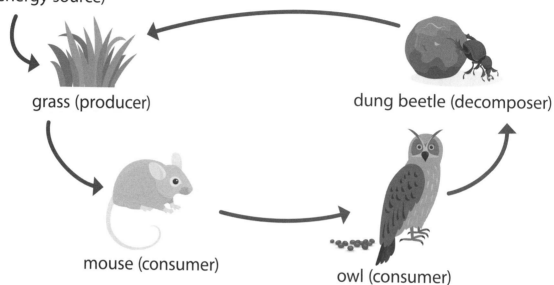

sun (energy source)

grass (producer)

dung beetle (decomposer)

mouse (consumer)

owl (consumer)

1. How does the mouse get energy?

_____

_____

_____

2. What is being decomposed?

_____

_____

3. Why is there an arrow between the decomposer and producer?

_____

_____

_____

Name: _____ **Date:** _____

Directions: Read the text. Then, summarize the challenge in your own words. Write any questions you have.

The Challenge

Teachers have an important job. They teach their students how to read and write. They show them how to do math and how to be critical thinkers. There are many science topics teacher cover, too! Teaching others is actually a great way to learn more about a topic. For this challenge, you will become the teacher. You will design a creative and informative lesson about the roles and importance of decomposers in food webs. Then, you will present your lesson to younger students.

Criteria

For your model ecosystem to be successful, it must…

- inform students about a food web with an energy source, a producer, two consumers, and a decomposer.
- highlight and explain the importance of decomposers.
- have a creative visual aid that is used during the presentation.

Constraints

- The presentation must be between two and three minutes long.
- You may only use the materials provided to you.

My Summary

_____

_____

_____

_____

My Questions

_____

_____

_____

Unit 6: Decomposers

Name: _____ Date: _____

Directions: Research decomposers you are interested in, and learn about the food webs they belong to. Answer the questions. Then, brainstorm and record ideas for your lesson and visual aid. Discuss ideas with others, and add to your brainstorming.

1. What types of decomposers are you most interested in? Circle one or two.

   bacteria   fungi   insects   worms

   crabs and lobsters   snails and slugs   other: _____

2. What habitats do these decomposers live in?

   _____

3. What will be the different parts of your food web?

   energy source: _____

   producer: _____

   consumer 1: _____

   consumer 2: _____

   decomposer: _____

My Brainstorming

_____

_____

_____

_____

_____

_____

_____

_____

Name: _____ Date: _____

Directions: Plan your lesson. Sketch one or more designs for your visual aid. Label the materials in your sketch. Then, answer the questions about your lesson.

1. What type of visual aid will you create?

poster   diorama   slideshow   other: _____

Lesson Plan

2. What are the main things you want students to learn from your lesson?

_____

_____

3. How will you explain the importance of decomposers in food webs?

_____

_____

4. How and when will you include your visual aid?

_____

_____

5. If you are working with others, what part will you do in the presentation?

_____

_____

Day 4

Name: _____ Date: _____

Directions: Gather your materials, plan your steps, and build your lesson plan visual aid. Record notes as you build. Then, practice giving your lesson a few times. Make sure you are within the time constraint.

Visual Aid Building Plan

	Job or Task	Group Member(s)
1		
2		
3		
4		
5		
6		

Building Notes
(additional steps, problems, changes, etc.)

Name: _____ **Date:** _____

Directions: Present your lesson to younger students. After you are finished, ask them the questions and record their answers.

1. What did you learn in the lesson?

_____

_____

_____

2. What are producers, consumers, and decomposers?

producers: _____

consumers: _____

decomposers: _____

3. Why are decomposers important?

_____

_____

_____

4. What was something you enjoyed about the lesson?

_____

_____

_____

5. How could we make the lesson more fun or interesting?

_____

_____

_____

Unit 6: Decomposers

Name: _____ Date: _____

Directions: Reflect on your design, and answer the questions. Then, plan how you will improve it. Conduct additional research if needed.

1. Did the students seem to understand what you were trying to teach them? Explain your answer.

   _____

   _____

   _____

2. What are some ways you could make your lesson more interesting, engaging, and/or clear?

   _____

   _____

   _____

The following criterion has been added to the lesson challenge:

- The visual aid must be interactive for the students. This means the students should do something with the visual aid during the lesson to learn.

---

3. What are some ways you could make your visual aid interactive?

   _____

   _____

   _____

Name: _____ Date: _____

Directions: Plan and sketch your new visual aid design. Label the parts and the materials you will use for each part. Then, answer the question.

In my redesign, I will...

add _____

remove _____

change _____

1. What changes will you make to your lesson?

_____

_____

_____

_____

Unit 6: Decomposers

Name: _____ Date: _____

Directions: Gather your materials, plan your steps, and rebuild your lesson plan visual aid. Record notes as you build. Then, practice giving your new lesson a few times. Make sure you are within the time constraint.

Visual Aid Rebuilding Plan

	Job or Task	Group Member(s)
1		
2		
3		
4		
5		
6		

Building Notes
(additional steps, problems, changes, etc.)

Name: _____ Date: _____

Directions: Present your lesson to a different group of students, if possible. After you are finished, ask them the questions and record their answers.

1. What did you learn in the lesson?

_____

_____

_____

2. What are producers, consumers, and decomposers?

_____

_____

_____

3. Why are decomposers important?

_____

_____

_____

4. What was something you enjoyed about the lesson?

_____

_____

_____

5. How could we make the lesson more fun or interesting?

_____

_____

_____

Day 5

Name: _____ Date: _____

Directions: Reflect on the work you did for this challenge. Answer the questions.

1. How did making the visual aid interactive change your presentation?

_____

_____

2. What did you enjoy about teaching the lesson?

_____

_____

3. What was challenging?

_____

_____

4. Did you learn anything about being a teacher? Explain your answer.

_____

_____

5. Draw yourself during a part of this challenge when you collaborated well with others. Write a caption telling what you are doing.

Living in Extremes Teaching Support

Overview of Unit Activities

Students will learn about and explore how animals live in extreme habitats through the following activities:

- reading about living in extreme habitats
- studying graphics about organisms in the deep sea
- experimenting to find out how colors affect heat absorption
- drawing creatures adapted to live in space
- analyzing a graph about melting polar ice sheets
- creating waterproof covers for an absorbent object

Materials Per Group

Week 1

- basic school supplies
- black and white paper
- clear glass bowl or jar
- heat lamp (or sun)
- thermometer

STEAM Challenge

- basic school supplies
- books or online resources about animals with waterproof adaptations
- fabric/material options (cotton, canvas, vinyl, plastic, etc.)
- oil
- packing tape
- plastic tub
- scale
- soft, absorbent object options (sponges, balled up socks, small stuffed animals, etc.)
- water
- wax
- wool yarn

Setup and Instructional Tips

- **STEAM Challenge:** The challenge can be done individually or in groups. Students working in groups should sketch their own designs first. Then, have them share designs in groups and choose one together.

- **Materials:** Students might ask for supplies not listed. Provide them with their requests if possible. Waxes and oils (particularly soybean and linseed) will help waterproof the uncovered part of the object during the redesign.

Discussion Questions

- What is an extreme habitat?
- What types of plants and animals live in extreme habitats?
- How can animals survive in extreme temperatures?
- What do humans do to survive in extreme temperatures?

Additional Notes

- **Possible Misconception:** Animal adaptations are only physical (such as thick fur or sharp claws).
  Truth: Some adaptations are behavioral (such as being nocturnal or migrating).
- **Possible Design Solutions:** Students may create waterproof coverings for their objects rather than putting them in plastic bags (or something similar).

Scaffolding and Extension Suggestions

- Assist students in researching different types of animals with adaptations for water. If necessary, share specific animals with them so they can conduct their research.
- Challenge students to look into methods of waterproofing already used for humans and attempt to incorporate that into their own designs.

Answer Key

Week 1 Day 1
1. C
2. D
3. B
4. A

Week 1 Day 2
1. A squishy body keeps the creature from being crushed by the pressure.
2. An anglerfish might not be able to find any food and it would die.
3. Responses should include students' opinions about which adaptations they find most interesting.

Week 1 Day 5
1. 1,250 Gt
2. Example: I predict the graph would show -2,800 Gt, because that is a difference of 400 Gt which seems to fit the pattern for the last few years.
3. Example: The animals might be able to find food more easily because the ground is showing instead of ice. The animals might not be able to stay safe because they can't blend into their surroundings without the white snow and ice.

Weeks 2 & 3
See STEAM Challenge Rubric on page 221.

Name: _____ **Date:** _____

Directions: Read the text, and choose the best answer for each question.

Extreme Habitats

Not every place on Earth has four seasons and moderate temperatures. Some habitats are considered extreme. This means they have intense features. Think of the tundra—it is extremely cold! Deserts can be very dry with hot temperatures. There is also the darkness of deep ocean trenches and the thin air at high altitudes.

Plants and animals live in these extreme habitats. They need adaptations to survive. Blubber or thick fur can keep animals warm. A plant might flourish in the heat because it does not need much water. Animals in deep ocean trenches might be adapted to live without sunlight. Animals living at high altitudes might have more blood vessels to pump oxygen through their bodies.

1. Which of these would *not* be considered an extreme habitat?
   - (A) tundra
   - (B) volcano
   - (C) forest
   - (D) desert

2. Which adaptation would help an animal in the desert?
   - (A) waterproof skin/fur
   - (B) thick fur to stay warm
   - (C) needing water every day
   - (D) nocturnal to avoid the sun

3. Why would animals need to adapt to living in high altitude habitats?
   - (A) It has warmer temperatures.
   - (B) It is harder to breathe.
   - (C) There is not enough sunlight.
   - (D) There are no plants.

4. Why would animals need to adapt to living in deep ocean trenches?
   - (A) There is no sunlight.
   - (B) There is no oxygen.
   - (C) There is no air pressure.
   - (D) There is no rain.

Unit 7: Living in Extremes

Name: _____ Date: _____

Directions: Read the text, and study the pictures. Then, answer the questions.

Surviving in Deep Ocean Trenches

Ocean trenches are the deepest parts on Earth. These areas have three main obstacles that creatures living there must overcome. The temperatures are nearly freezing. No sunlight can reach the bottom. The pressure is eight tons per square inch. (That means 16,000 pounds is pressing down on one square inch of the ocean floor.) Some animals have adapted to live in the deepest ocean trenches. They are unique, to say the least.

This is a grenadier (rattail) fish. It has a slow metabolism, which helps it conserve energy so it does not get too cold.

This is a humpback anglerfish. The pole on its head makes its own light to attract prey or find a mate.

This is a deep-sea jellyfish. Its squishy, boneless body helps it to not get crushed under the high pressure.

1. How does a squishy body help animals live in the deep ocean?

   _____

   _____

2. What might happen to a humpback anglerfish if its light did not work?

   _____

   _____

3. Which adaptation do you think is most interesting? Why?

   _____

   _____

Name: _____   Date: _____

Directions: Follow the steps to investigate how color affects heat absorption.

Question: Will the color of background paper affect the temperature of water?

Materials

black paper	clear bowl or jar	heat lamp
thermometer	water	white paper

Steps

1. Cover the bottoms of two clear bowls or jars with water. Take and record their temperatures.

2. Place the first bowl on black paper, and put it under a heat lamp for five minutes. Take and record the temperature.

3. Place the second bowl on white paper, and put it under the heat lamp for five minutes. Take and record the temperature.

Results

	Starting Temperature	Ending Temperature
black paper	_____ °F _____ °C	_____ °F _____ °C
white paper	_____ °F _____ °C	_____ °F _____ °C

Talk About It!

Did the background color make a difference? How could this information be applied to animals who live in the desert? If you were going somewhere hot, what would you wear? Why?

Name: _____ Date: _____

Directions: Outer space would definitely be an extreme habitat! Draw a creature who is able to live in space. It should have at least three adaptations. Then, explain your drawing.

_____

_____

_____

_____

Day 5

Name: _____ **Date:** _____

Directions: Read the text, and study the graph. Then, answer the questions.

Shrinking Ice Sheets

Antarctica is an extreme habitat with an extreme problem. Its polar ice sheets are melting. An ice sheet is a permanent layer of ice covering an area of land. Scientists believe the melting is caused by climate change. The mass of the ice sheets is measured in gigatons (Gt). A metric ton is 1,000 kg, and a gigaton is a billion metric tons. As the ice sheets melt, their mass decreases. Scientists keep track of how much the sheets have lost.

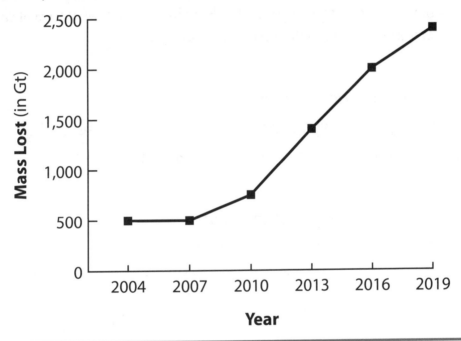

1. How many gigatons were lost between 2010 and 2016? _____

2. What number would you predict for the year 2022? Explain your answer.

   _____

   _____

3. How could the melting of polar ice sheets affect animals living in Antarctica?

   _____

   _____

Day 1

Name: _____ Date: _____

Directions: Read the text. Then, summarize the challenge in your own words. Write any questions you have.

The Challenge

Some animals live only on land, and others only in the water. But some animals spend a lot of time in both places. For this reason, they have special adaptations. They need to be waterproof or water resistant. If a human or land animal was going to spend time in an extreme habitat, such as a tundra or ocean, they would need help surviving. A company wants to mimic animal waterproofing for people. For this challenge, you will design a waterproof covering for a small, absorbent object.

Criteria

For the waterproof design to be successful, it must…

- keep the object dry when submerged in water for 5 seconds.
- be a covering that accommodates the size of the object.

Constraints

- The object cannot be placed into a bag.
- You may only use the materials provided to you.

My Summary

_____

_____

_____

_____

My Questions

_____

_____

_____

_____

Name: _____ **Date:** _____

Directions: Research waterproof adaptations for animals, and answer the questions. Then, brainstorm and record ideas for creating a waterproof covering. Discuss ideas with others, and add to your brainstorming.

1. List one reptile or amphibian that lives in the water and on land. What adaptations does it have for being in the water?

   _____

   _____

2. List a mammal that lives on land, but spends a lot of time in the water. What adaptations do they have for the water?

   _____

   _____

3. List a bird that spends time on both land and in water. What adaptations does it have for the water?

   _____

   _____

My Brainstorming

_____

_____

_____

_____

_____

_____

_____

_____

Day 3

Name: _____ Date: _____

Directions: Sketch one or more designs for your waterproof covering. Label the parts and the object you will protect. List the materials. Then, answer the question.

Materials

_____   _____   _____

_____   _____   _____

1. Which animal's adaptation do you think your design mimicks most closely? Explain your answer.

_____

_____

Name: _____ Date: _____

Directions: Gather your materials, plan your steps, and build your waterproof covering design. Record notes as you build.

Waterproof Covering Building Plan

	Job or Task	Group Member(s)
1		
2		
3		
4		
5		
6		

Building Notes
(additional steps, problems, changes, etc.)

Talk About It!

How do you think your covering will work?
Do you predict any problems? Why or why not?

Unit 7: Living in Extremes

Name: _____ Date: _____

Directions: Follow the steps to test your waterproof covering. Record your results. Then, answer the question.

1. Weigh your object without its covering. Record the weight and your observations.

2. Put the covering on your object.

3. Submerge your object in water for five seconds. You may hold it under water or put something on it to weigh it down.

4. Weigh your object without its covering after it comes out of the water. Record the weight and your observations.

	Weight (in grams)	Weight (in ounces)	Observations
Before			
After			

5. How much water did your object absorb?

_____

Name: _____ Date: _____

Directions: Reflect on your design, and answer the questions. Then, plan how you will improve it. Conduct additional research if needed.

1. What parts and materials worked well for your covering?

_____

_____

_____

2. What flaws did you notice that need to be fixed?

_____

_____

_____

Draw a star next to one or more ways you will improve your design.

- My first design did not meet all the criteria. To improve it, I will

_____

_____

_____

- Accept a new challenge—You must leave a 1 cm (0.4 inch) square uncovered on the object. The uncovered square can be treated with something to help it be more waterproof, but it cannot be the same material as the covering.

- Build a covering that will work on a larger object.

- My own idea: _____

_____

_____

Name: _____ Date: _____

Directions: Plan and sketch your new waterproof covering design. Label the parts and the materials you will use for each part. Then, answer the question.

In my redesign, I will...

add _____

remove _____

change _____

1. What are some possible pros and cons to your design changes?

_____

_____

Name: _____ Date: _____

Directions: Gather your materials. Answer the question, plan your steps, and rebuild your waterproof covering design. Record notes as you build.

1. What did you learn from building the first design that you can apply as you rebuild?

   _____

   _____

Waterproof Covering Rebuilding Plan

	Job or Task	Group Member(s)
1		
2		
3		
4		
5		
6		

Building Notes
(additional steps, problems, changes, etc.)

Name: _____ Date: _____

Directions: Follow the steps to test your new waterproof covering. Record your results, and answer the questions.

1. Weigh your object without its covering. Record the weight and write down your observations.

2. Put the covering on your object.

3. Submerge your object in water for five seconds. You may hold it under water or put something on it to weigh it down.

4. Weigh your object without its covering after it comes out of the water. Record the weight and write down your observations.

	Weight (in grams)	**Weight** (in ounces)	**Observations**
Before			
After			

5. How much water did your object absorb?

   _____

6. Did your new design work better? What is your evidence and reasoning?

   _____

   _____

   _____

   _____

Name: _____ Date: _____

Directions: Answer the questions to reflect on your waterproof covering.

1. Would you consider your waterproofing a success? What is your evidence or reasoning?

   _____

   _____

2. Why would people need ways to stay waterproof or to keep items from getting wet?

   _____

   _____

3. How does this challenge compare to real-life examples of waterproofing you have seen?

   _____

   _____

4. Draw yourself living in an extreme environment. Write a caption telling what you are doing.

+ −
× ÷

```



```

Primary Producers Teaching Support

Overview of Unit Activities

Students will learn about and explore primary producers through the following activities:

- reading about primary producers
- studying a flowchart about energy
- experimenting with photosynthesis by creating oxygen
- drawing primary producers observed on a nature walk
- analyzing a food web flowchart
- creating pots for different types of seeds

Materials Per Group

Week 1

- baking soda ($\frac{1}{4}$ tsp., 1 g)
- basic school supplies
- clear jar/beaker
- elodea (or other aquatic plants, available online or at pet/aquatic stores)
- lamp
- rocks
- water

STEAM Challenge

- air-dry clay/dough
- basic school supplies
- books or online resources about home herb garden kits
- cardboard tubes (4–5)
- craft sticks (10–15)
- fresh herb seed options (rosemary, mint, cilantro, thyme, oregano, etc.)
- other recyclable materials (cardboard, egg cartons, glass jars, etc.)
- paper or plastic cups (various sizes)
- paper towels
- pipe cleaners (10–15)
- plastic bottles (4–8)
- shoebox
- soil
- string or yarn (4–5 feet, 1.5 m)

Setup and Instructional Tips

- **STEAM Challenge:** The challenge can be done individually or in groups. Students working in groups should sketch their own designs first. Then, have them share designs in groups and choose one together.

Discussion Questions

- How are plants different from animals?
- How do plants make food?
- What would happen to the food web if there were no plants?
- What problems do farmers and gardeners have today?

Additional Notes

- **Possible Misconception:** Plants have to have sunlight to grow.
  Truth: In many situations, plants can use artificial lights to accomplish photosynthesis.
- **Possible Design Solutions:** Have students label craft sticks with the names of the herbs they are growing and stick them in the soil by the seeds.

Scaffolding and Extension Suggestions

- Preview vocabulary with students before beginning the unit, and encourage students to write down words they want to remember and then illustrate their meanings.
- Challenge students to learn about phytoremediation (using plants to help clean up environmental contamination).
- When the challenge is complete, encourage students to continue taking care of their plants. If possible, keep them at school for a few weeks to continue watching them grow.

Answer Key

Week 1 Day 1
1. A
2. D
3. A
4. C

Week 1 Day 2
1. Hydroponics is growing plants using water and light, no soil.
2. Example: Plants growing anywhere is an important advantage because plants can usually only grow in certain places with good soil.
3. Example: Expensive equipment is an important disadvantage because it is hard for people to save and buy materials for a new project when they could garden in soil for less money.

Week 1 Day 5
1. primary producers
2. A human could be a primary consumer if they were a vegetarian or a secondary consumer if they also ate animals.
3. Answers should include herbivores, such as cows, horses, and rabbits.

Weeks 2 & 3
See STEAM Challenge Rubric on page 221.

Unit 8: Primary Producers

Name: _____ Date: _____

Directions: Read the text, and study the diagram. Then, choose the best answer for each question.

Primary Producers

The sun is the start of all energy on Earth. It provides light and heat for humans. The sun also provides a vital part of plants' survival. Plants need three things to create their own food. They are light, water, and carbon dioxide (a gas). This process is called photosynthesis. Since plants can produce their own food, they are called primary producers. Humans and animals have an important relationship with plants. Plants make oxygen, a gas, during photosynthesis. Humans and animals breathe in oxygen. Then, they exhale carbon dioxide. The plants use carbon dioxide in their process of making food.

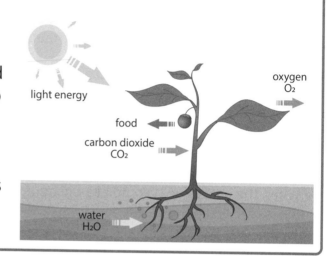

1. What is photosynthesis?

   (A) when a plant makes its food

   (B) when oxygen turns into carbon dioxide

   (C) when carbon dioxide turns into water

   (D) when animals exhale a gas plants need

2. Why is the sun important for photosynthesis?

   (A) It provides people with oxygen.

   (B) It provides plants with heat.

   (C) It provides people with energy.

   (D) It provides plants with light.

3. Which of these is released during photosynthesis?

   (A) oxygen

   (B) carbon dioxide

   (C) water

   (D) sunlight

4. Why are plants called primary producers?

   (A) They supply oxygen to people.

   (B) They produce food for animals.

   (C) They make their own food.

   (D) They depend on the sun.

Name: _____ **Date:** _____

Directions: Read the text, and study the chart. Then, answer the questions.

Hydroponics

People often think a plant needs water, sunlight, and soil to grow. But only two of those are really necessary! Soil is not needed. Growing plants with water and light is called hydroponics. The concept has been used for thousands of years, but became more common in the 1940s. Its popularity has really increased in the last 20 years. There are good and bad things about hydroponics.

Advantages	Disadvantages
• Plants grow faster and yield more crops. • There are fewer pests. • The plants can be grown anywhere. • Less water is needed than with soil farming (because the water is recycled).	• Waterborne diseases spread quickly. • The equipment is expensive. • The plants need more supervision than with soil farming. • More training and knowledge are needed.

1. What does *hydroponics* mean?

_____

_____

2. Which advantage do you think is most important? Why?

_____

_____

3. Which disadvantage do you think is most significant? Why?

_____

_____

Unit 8: Primary Producers

Day 3

Name: _____ Date: _____

Directions: Follow the steps to complete an experiment about photosynthesis.

> **Question:** How do plants make oxygen during photosynthesis?

Materials

baking soda (source of carbon dioxide)	clear jar/beaker
elodea (aquatic plant) lamp	rocks water

Steps

1. Mix 2 cups (500 mL) of water with $\frac{1}{4}$ teaspoon (1 g) of baking soda.

2. Place at least 18 inches (45 cm) of elodea in the bottom of the jar and place a rock on top to weigh it down.

3. Pour the baking soda and water over the plant.

4. Keeping the light off, count how many air bubbles come to the surface of the water during five minutes. Record your answer.

5. Turn on the lamp light and place the jar under the lamp. Count how many air bubbles come to the surface of the water during five minutes. Record your answer.

Results

Bubbles in the dark: _____

Bubbles in the light: _____

Talk About It!

What were the bubbles made of? How does this compare with photosynthesis? How might the experiment be different using the sun instead of a lamp?

Name: _____ **Date:** _____

Directions: Go on a nature walk. Draw three different plants, flowers, or leaves you find. Try to find out their names if you don't know them!

Day 5

Name: _____ Date: _____

Directions: Study the flowchart, and answer the questions.

The Flow of Energy

The Sun
The sun gives energy to plants. It is the beginning of all food webs.

Primary Producers
Plants use sunlight, water, and carbon dioxide to make their food. The process is called photosynthesis.

Primary Consumers
Some animals eat only plants. They depend on them for food because they cannot make their own.

Secondary Consumers
Some animals eat other animals. They might also eat plants.

1. Which organism in this flowchart uses carbon dioxide? _____

2. Which organisms in the flowchart could a human be? Explain your answer.

_____

_____

3. List at least three animals that are primary consumers.

_____

_____

Name: _____ Date: _____

Directions: Read the text. Then, summarize the challenge in your own words. Write any questions you have.

The Challenge

Home gardening is very popular. Most people think of a garden with only fruits, vegetables, or flowers, but these can take a long time to grow and need a lot of space. Herbs are a great alternative. Using fresh herbs is great for cooking and consuming, and many kinds can even be grown indoors. For this challenge, you will design a mini herb garden planter for a local garden store to sell.

Criteria

For the design to be successful, it must…

- have places for four different types of herb plants to grow.
- have labels for each plant.
- be able to be carried all together.
- have a unique design or decorations that customers will enjoy.

Constraints

- The herb garden must be made using at least one recycled material.
- You may only use the materials provided to you.

My Summary

_____

_____

_____

My Questions

_____

_____

_____

Unit 8: Primary Producers

Name: _____ Date: _____

Directions: Research different herbs and how to grow them, and answer the questions. Then, brainstorm and record ideas. Discuss ideas with others, and add to your brainstorming.

1. Think of a few of your favorite meals or desserts, and read their recipes. What herbs do they use?

   _____

   _____

2. What type of planters or containers would work well for your herbs? Think about size, shape, and materials.

   _____

   _____

3. Find some examples of small herb gardens or kits for indoors. Draw two examples.

Example 1	Example 2

My Brainstorming

_____

_____

_____

_____

_____

_____

Day 3

Name: _____ Date: _____

Directions: Sketch one or more designs for your mini herb garden planter design. List the materials. Then, answer the question.

Materials

_____ _____ _____

_____ _____ _____

1. What part of your design plan are you most excited about?

_____

_____

Day 4

Name: _____ Date: _____

Directions: Gather your materials, plan your steps, and build your mini herb garden planter. Record notes as you build.

Herb Garden Building Plan

	Job or Task	Group Member(s)
1		
2		
3		
4		
5		
6		

Building Notes
(additional steps, problems, changes, etc.)

Quick Tip!

It is okay to do a few mini tests as you build! Make sure all the parts stay together when you pick up and carry the planter.

Name: _____ Date: _____

Directions: Evaluate your herb garden using the table. Explain or elaborate on your responses in the Notes column.

My Herb Garden Design...	Notes
has at least four herbs planted. yes no	
uses at least one recycled material. yes no	
has the herbs labeled. yes no	
can be picked up and carried as one unit. yes no	
has designs or decorations that customers will enjoy. yes no	

Unit 8: Primary Producers

Name: _____ Date: _____

Directions: Reflect on your design, and answer the questions. Then, plan how you will improve it. Conduct additional research if needed.

1. What went well in creating your garden?

   _____

   _____

   _____

2. What flaws did you observe in your design?

   _____

   _____

   _____

> The following constraint has been changed:
>
> • Your mini herb garden design must be made with at least three recycled materials.

3. What other goals or challenges do you want to set for your second design?

   _____

   _____

   _____

Day 2

Name: _____ Date: _____

Directions: Plan and sketch your new mini herb garden design. Label the parts and the materials you will use for each part. Then, complete the sentence.

In my redesign, I will…

add _____

remove _____

change _____

1. The change or improvement I am most excited about is _____

_____

_____

Unit 8: Primary Producers

Name: _____ Date: _____

Directions: Gather your materials, plan your steps, and rebuild your mini herb garden planter. Record notes as you build.

Herb Garden Rebuilding Plan

	Job or Task	Group Member(s)
1		
2		
3		
4		
5		
6		

Building Notes
(additional steps, changes, improvements, etc.)

Name: _____ Date: _____

Day 4

Directions: Evaluate your herb garden using the table. Explain or elaborate on your responses in the Notes column.

My Herb Garden Design...	Notes
has at least four herbs planted. yes no	
uses at least three recycled materials. yes no	
has the herbs labeled. yes no	
can be picked up and carried as one unit. yes no	
has designs or decorations that customers will enjoy. yes no	

Name: _____ Date: _____

Directions: Answer the questions to reflect on your herb garden.

1. What did you enjoy about creating your herb garden? What was a challenge?

_____

_____

_____

_____

_____

2. Do you think you will continue your herb garden at home? Why or why not?

_____

_____

_____

_____

3. What benefits are there to growing your own herbs?

_____

_____

_____

_____

_____

_____

Try This!

Take your herb garden home and use the herbs in your favorite recipes. Think about how the energy from the sun is being passed on to you when you consume, or eat, the herbs.

Earth in Motion Teaching Support

Overview of Unit Activities

Students will learn about and explore Earth's movement through the following activities:

- reading about Earth's motion in a day, month, and year
- observing graphics about constellations
- experimenting with shadows over time
- creating pictures with shadows created by the sun
- studying the differences between solar and lunar eclipses
- building working sundials

Materials Per Group

Week 1

- basic school supplies
- masking tape
- measuring tape or ruler

- toys or figurines to trace shadows
- wooden stakes (or poles, dowels, etc.)

STEAM Challenge

- basic school supplies
- books or online resources about sundials
- clay, dough, and plaster of paris
- compass
- paper plates

- plastic plates
- rocks
- straws
- unsharpened pencils

Setup and Instructional Tips

- **Week 1 Day 3 and Testing Days:** These days involve several brief trips outside. They also require sunny days. If Daylight Savings Time is currently being observed, keep in mind that the sun will actually be at its highest point at 1:00 p.m.
- **STEAM Challenge:** The challenge can be done individually or in groups. Students working in groups should sketch their own designs first. Then, have them share designs in groups and choose one together.

Discussion Questions

- Why do we have day and night on Earth?
- What things in space move? Which do not?
- How do shadows change throughout the day?
- How do people know what time it is?

Additional Notes

- **Possible Misconception:** Daytime and nighttime are equal lengths of time.
  Truth: Due to Earth's tilt and its revolution around the sun, the amount of daylight and nighttime a location has depends on the time of year.
- **Possible Design Solutions:** Students might make sundials with paper plates and pencil/straws. They may choose to use plastic plates or wooden disks, or to make the bases from clay, dough, or plaster of paris.

Scaffolding and Extension Suggestions

- Use a light source and ball to demonstrate day and night for students who are struggling to understand Earth's rotation.
- Challenge students to set their sundial even more accurately by finding the latitude of their city and learning how to adjust their sundials accordingly.

Answer Key

Week 1 Day 1
1. B
2. A
3. D
4. C

Week 1 Day 2
1. People can't see all the constellations because of where they are on Earth or because of where Earth is in its revolution around the sun.
2. People can see both from the equator because it is in the middle.
3. Example: People grouped the stars because it made them easier to find and remember.

Week 1 Day 5
1. Example: Solar eclipses have the moon between the sun and Earth. Lunar eclipses have Earth between the sun and moon.
2. Both types of eclipses create a shadow that looks like a dark circle.
3. The eclipses are not visible to everyone because they are on different places on Earth.

Weeks 2 & 3
See STEAM Challenge Rubric on page 221.

Name: _____ Date: _____

Directions: Read the text, and study the diagram. Then, choose the best answer for each question.

Earth's Movement

The Earth moves in two distinct ways—it rotates and revolves. An imaginary pole called an axis runs through Earth at the North and South Poles. Earth rotates (or spins) around its axis. This takes 24 hours, or one complete day. Half of the Earth is facing the sun, so it is daytime there. The other side is facing away from the sun, so it is night there.

The moon revolves around Earth, which means it moves around Earth in a circle-like pattern. This takes about one month. During that time, different parts of the moon are visible.

Earth revolves around the sun which takes 365 days, or one complete year. As the Earth revolves, it goes through different seasons. Different constellations are visible, too.

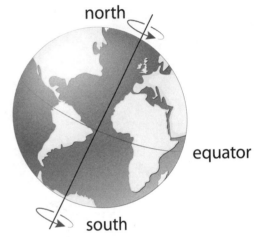

1. You experience night when _____.
   - (A) you are facing the sun
   - (B) you are facing away from the sun
   - (C) you are facing the moon
   - (D) you are facing away from the moon

2. Earth _____ on its axis.
   - (A) rotates
   - (B) revolves
   - (C) moves
   - (D) runs

3. How long does it take the moon to revolve around Earth?
   - (A) one day
   - (B) one week
   - (C) one year
   - (D) one month

4. Why are different constellations visible during the year?
   - (A) The moon is revolving around Earth.
   - (B) The stars are moving.
   - (C) Earth is revolving around the sun.
   - (D) The sun is shining differently on them.

Name: _____ **Date:** _____

Directions: Read the text, and study the diagram. Then, answer the questions.

Constellations

Constellations are groups of stars. People group them together to make pictures. People cannot always see all constellations. Their location in space makes a difference. So does Earth's location as it revolves around the sun. The diagram shows Earth and two famous constellations. Ursa Major is easily seen north of the equator. The Southern Cross is easily seen south of the equator.

Ursa Major

equator

Southern Cross

1. Why can't people see all the constellations from one location?

   _____

   _____

2. Where could people probably see both constellations? Explain your answer.

   _____

   _____

3. Why do you think people grouped the stars into pictures?

   _____

   _____

Name: _____ Date: _____

Directions: Follow the steps to complete an activity about shadows.

> **Question:** What happens to shadows during the day?

> **Materials**
>
> masking tape   measuring tape   wooden stake

Steps

1. In the morning, put the stake in the ground in a clear space. You should be able to see its shadow.

2. Put tape on the shadow to show its length and location. Measure and record the length of the shadow. Leave the tape throughout the activity.

3. Repeat Step 2 four more times throughout the day. If possible, space out the visits so they are an hour apart.

4. Draw the stake and masking tape strips as they appear at the end of the activity.

Results

	Drawing
Time: _____ Length: _____	
Time: _____ Length: _____	
Time: _____ Length: _____	
Time: _____ Length: _____	
Time: _____ Length: _____	

Talk About It!

What happened to the shadows during the day? Why?

What does this show you about Earth's movement?

How could you use shadows to tell time?

Day 4

Name: _____ Date: _____

Directions: Make a picture using shadows created by the sun. Go outside in the morning or afternoon. Place different toys and figures on and around your paper. Trace their shadows on your paper. Move them around and trace more shadows if you want.

Name: _____ Date: _____

Directions: Read about eclipses, and study the diagrams. Then, answer the questions.

Solar Eclipse	Lunar Eclipse
A solar eclipse happens when the moon is between the sun and Earth. The sun looks like it is completely or partially covered with a dark circle.	A lunar eclipse happens when Earth is between the moon and sun. Earth's shadow is on the moon, so the moon looks like it is covered with a dark circle.
sun moon Earth	sun Earth moon

1. How are solar and lunar eclipses different?

   _____

   _____

   _____

2. How are solar and lunar eclipses similar?

   _____

   _____

   _____

3. When a solar or lunar eclipse happens, it is not visible to everyone on Earth. Why do you think that happens?

   _____

   _____

   _____

Day 1

Name: _____ Date: _____

Directions: Read the text. Then, summarize the challenge in your own words. Write any questions you have.

The Challenge

Long before watches, digital clocks, and cell phones, people knew the time. They used sundials! Sundials are still used today. They can be helpful if you find yourself without modern technology. Imagine you are headed to a technology-free campout. For this challenge, create a sundial that could be used at the campsite.

Criteria

For the design to be successful, it must…

- give the correct time to the nearest hour.
- include unique drawings, designs, or shapes to represent a theme of your choosing.

Constraint

- You may only use the materials provided to you.

My Summary

_____

_____

_____

_____

My Questions

_____

_____

_____

_____

Name: _____ Date: _____

Directions: Research sundials, and answer the questions. Then, brainstorm and record ideas. Discuss ideas with others, and add to your brainstorming.

1. When did people start using sundials? _____

2. What are the two main parts of a sundial?

_____   _____

3. How do sundials work?

_____

_____

4. What are some examples you found of unique sundial designs?

_____

_____

_____

_____

_____

```
My Brainstorming
_____
_____
_____
_____
_____
_____
_____
_____
_____
```

Unit 9: Earth in Motion

Name: _____ Date: _____

Directions: Sketch one or more designs for your sundial. Show how it will use shadows to show the time. List the materials. Then, answer the question.

Materials

_____   _____   _____

_____   _____   _____

1. What theme did you choose to represent in your sundial? What designs or decorations do you plan to include?

_____

_____

Day 4

Name: _____ Date: _____

Directions: Gather your materials, plan your steps, and build your sundial. Record notes as you build.

Sundial Building Plan

	Job or Task	Group Member(s)
1		
2		
3		
4		
5		
6		

Building Notes
(additional steps, surprises, changes, etc.)

Talk About It!

How will you set up your sundial on the ground? How can you make sure your sundial is as accurate as possible? How will you read the sundial?

Unit 9: Earth in Motion

Name: _____ Date: _____

Directions: Set up your sundial outside in the morning. Check on it four times during the day. Record the time and draw your sundial during each time. Then, answer the question.

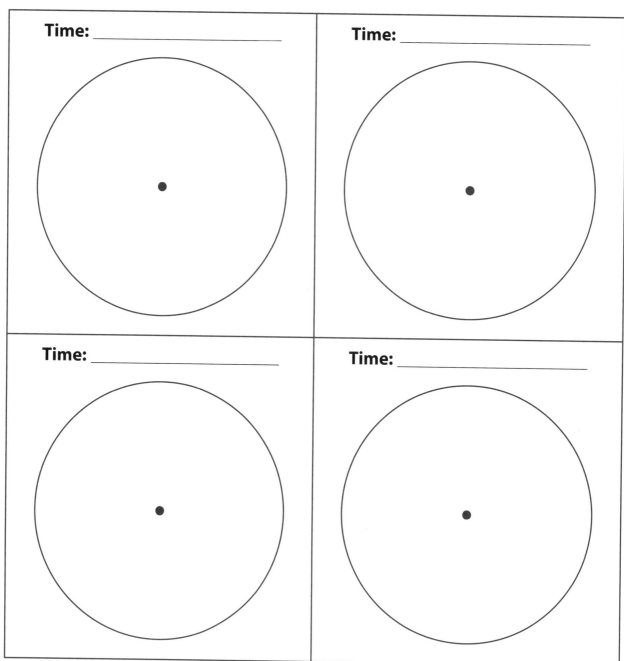

Time: _____

Time: _____

Time: _____

Time: _____

1. Describe the designs or decorations you included to represent the theme.

_____

_____

🔬 Day 1

Name: _____ Date: _____

Directions: Reflect on your design, and answer the questions. Then, plan how you will improve it. Conduct additional research if needed.

1. What went well with your sundial?

_____

_____

_____

2. What about your design did not work as well as it should have?

_____

_____

_____

Draw a star next to one or more ways you will improve your design.

- My first design did not meet all the criteria. To improve it, I will

  _____

  _____

- Include a traditional *gnomon* in the design. Research to learn what this is and how you might incorporate it.

- My own idea: _____

  _____

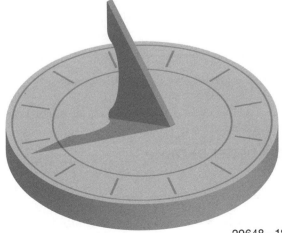

Day 2

Name: _____ Date: _____

Directions: Plan and sketch your new sundial design. Label the parts and the materials you will use for each part. Then, complete the sentence.

In my redesign, I will...

add _____

remove _____

change _____

1. This design will work better because _____

_____

Name: _____ **Date:** _____

Directions: Gather your materials, plan your steps, and rebuild your sundial. Record notes as you build.

Sundial Rebuilding Plan

	Job or Task	Group Member(s)
1		
2		
3		
4		
5		
6		

Building Notes
(additional steps, surprises, changes, etc.)

Day 4

Name: _____ Date: _____

Directions: Set up your sundial outside in the morning. Check on it four times during the day. Record the time and draw your sundial during each time. Then, answer the question.

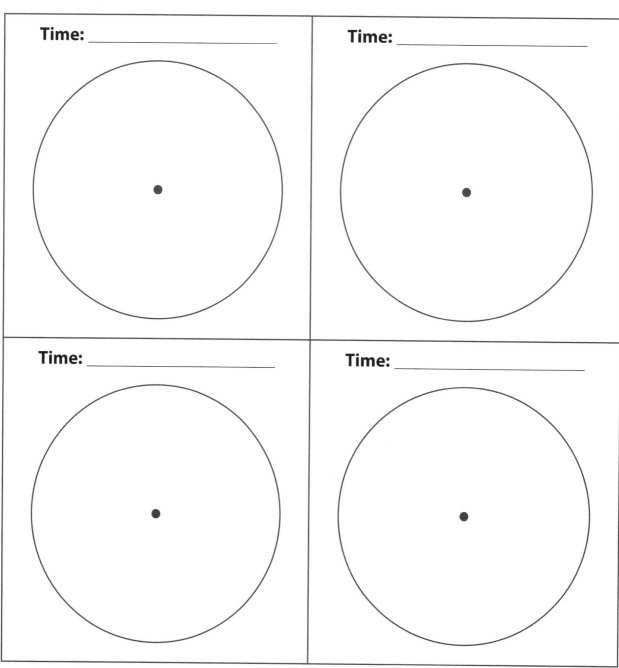

Time: _____

Time: _____

Time: _____

Time: _____

1. Did your second sundial design work better? What is your evidence?

_____

_____

Name: _____ Date: _____

Directions: Reflect on the work you did for this challenge, and answer the questions.

1. What similarities do you notice between sundials and watches or clocks?

_____

_____

_____

2. Did you notice any problems telling time on a sundial? Explain your answer.

_____

_____

_____

3. Why do you think people today still want to own sundials?

_____

_____

_____

4. What are you most proud of about this challenge?

_____

_____

_____

Hurricanes Teaching Support

Overview of Unit Activities

Students will learn about and explore hurricanes through the following activities:

- reading about hurricanes
- studying a flowchart about how hurricanes form
- experimenting with how hurricanes look
- drawing pictures of a bird's-eye view of the eye of a hurricane
- observing a map showing hurricane locations
- creating hurricane-proof structures

Materials Per Group

Week 1

- basic school supplies
- clear bowl or wide-mouth clear jar
- food coloring
- spoon
- water

STEAM Challenge

- basic school supplies
- books or online resources about hurricanes
- cardboard (4–5 sheets)
- cardstock (4–5 sheets)
- craft sticks (10–15)
- fan with at least three speeds
- foam board
- modeling clay or dough
- ruler
- shower curtain or tarp (optional)
- spray bottle
- straws (5–10)
- toothpicks (10–15)
- wooden dowels/skewers (5–10)

Setup and Instructional Tips

- **STEAM Challenge:** The challenge can be done individually or in groups. Students working in groups should sketch their own designs first. Then, have them share designs in groups and choose one together.

- **Testing Days:** There is potential for floors to get wet. If possible, put down a shower curtain or tarp when testing the structures to keep the floor dry.

Discussion Questions

- What is a hurricane?
- Where do hurricanes happen? Why?
- Why are hurricanes dangerous?
- How do people prepare for hurricanes?

Additional Notes

- **Possible Misconception:** Atlantic hurricanes only happen during hurricane season (June–November).
  Truth: Most hurricanes happen then, but there has been at least one hurricane reported in each month.
- **Possible Design Solutions:** Students may attach their structures to the plate with clay or dough.

Scaffolding and Extension Suggestions

- Allow students to look at videos or pictures of hurricane-safe structures to give them ideas on how to build their structures.
- Encourage students to look into architecture and see how to strengthen their structure.

Answer Key

Week 1 Day 1
1. A
2. D
3. B
4. D

Week 1 Day 2
1. Air above the ocean is heated and rises. As it rises higher, it begins to cool. This causes water vapor to condense and form storm clouds.
2. The clouds turn because Earth is rotating.
3. Hurricanes cannot form in cold ocean water because the cold water will not heat up the air above it and make it rise.

Week 1 Day 5
1. Florida, Texas, Louisiana; 235 hurricanes total
2. Southern states have more hurricanes because they are warmer, and hurricanes need warm water to form.
3. If ocean temperatures rise, there will be more hurricanes in the northern states because the warmer water is needed to form the storms.

Weeks 2 & 3
See STEAM Challenge Rubric on page 221.

Unit 10: Hurricanes

Name: _____ Date: _____

Directions: Read the text, and choose the best answer for each question.

Hurricanes

Tropical cyclones are large, destructive storms. They form over ocean water near the equator. In some places they are called typhoons or cyclones. When they occur over the Atlantic or eastern Pacific Oceans, they are called hurricanes. Many hurricanes stay in the open ocean. These storms do not affect people on land. However, when a hurricane hits land, it is dangerous. Strong winds and heavy rains cause flooding and destroy buildings. People can even die in them. Most states along the American east coast have been hit by hurricanes. Florida, Texas, and Louisiana have had the most.

The Saffir-Simpson scale is used to rate hurricanes. They are given a number 1–5. The smallest storms are rated a 1, and the most destructive ones are rated a 5. Category 5 hurricanes have wind speeds of at least 157 mph (253 km/h).

1. Where do hurricanes form?
   - (A) near the equator
   - (B) near the poles
   - (C) over land
   - (D) in the deep sea

2. Are all hurricanes dangerous to people on land?
   - (A) Yes, because they cause flooding.
   - (B) No, because some are too small to cause damage.
   - (C) Yes, because they cannot be predicted.
   - (D) No, because some stay in the open ocean.

3. Which state would *not* be hit by a hurricane? (You may look at a map.)
   - (A) North Carolina
   - (B) Oklahoma
   - (C) Virginia
   - (D) Georgia

4. Which hurricane would be considered the most dangerous?
   - (A) Category 1
   - (B) Category 2
   - (C) Category 4
   - (D) Category 5

Name: _____ Date: _____

Directions: Read the text, and study the diagram. Then, answer the questions.

Hurricane Formation

Hurricanes are formed over warm ocean water. The moist air above the water is warm, so it rises. Cooler air moves in to takes its place. The warm air rises and begins to cool high in the atmosphere. Water vapor condenses and forms storm clouds. The clouds begin turning because Earth is rotating. When these steps happen over and over, the clouds get very big and wind speeds increase. When wind speeds reach 74 mph, a storm is officially a hurricane.

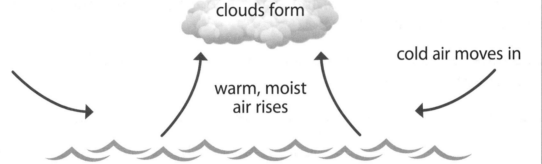

clouds form

cold air moves in

warm, moist
air rises

warm ocean water
(80 degrees Fahrenheit or greater)

---

1. What causes storm clouds to form?

_____

_____

_____

2. Why do the clouds begin turning?

_____

_____

3. Could a hurricane form in a cold part of the ocean? Why or why not?

_____

_____

Unit 10: Hurricanes

Name: _____ Date: _____

Directions: Follow the steps to investigate how hurricanes move.

> **Question:** What do hurricanes look like as they move?

> ### Materials
> clear bowl   food coloring   spoon   water

Steps

1. Fill up the bowl a little over halfway with water.

2. Use the spoon to quickly stir the water. Keep the spoon in the middle, and stir in a small, tight circle.

3. Remove the spoon and immediately put a drop of food coloring in the center of the water.

4. Observe what happens from above. Record your observations.

5. Pour out the water, and do the steps again. Observe from the side of the bowl. Record your observations.

Results

Drawing from the Top	Drawing from the Side

Talk About It!

How do you think this shows what happens to a hurricane over time?

What did you notice about the center of the "hurricane"?

Name: _____ **Date:** _____

Directions: Read about the eye of a hurricane. Then, draw a bird's-eye view of what a hurricane looks like.

> The eye of a hurricane is the very center. It is actually the calmest part of the storm. It is an area of low pressure. The eye is usually 20–40 miles (32–64 km) across. The eyewall surrounds the eye. This is where the storm is worst.

Day 5

Name: _____ Date: _____

Directions: Study the map. It shows how many hurricanes hit land in the U.S. between the years 1851 and 2017. Then, answer the questions.

Number of Hurricanes per State (1851–2017)

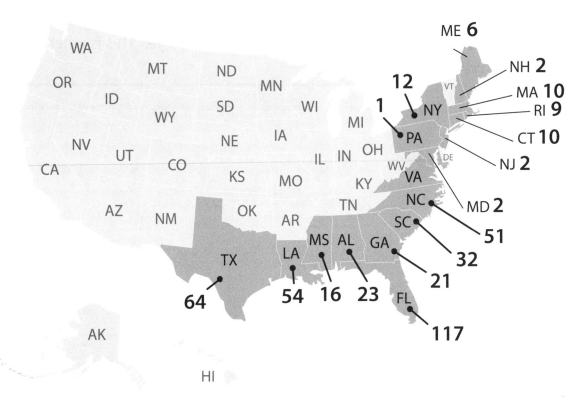

1. Which three states have had the most hurricanes? How many hurricanes do they have combined?

   _____   _____   _____

   _____

2. Do states in the north or the south have more hurricanes? Why do you think that is?

   _____

   _____

3. If ocean temperatures rise, how could that affect the number of hurricanes? Explain your answer.

   _____

   _____

Day 1

Name: _____ **Date:** _____

Directions: Read the text. Then, summarize the challenge in your own words. Write any questions you have.

The Challenge

High winds and heavy rains are problems when hurricanes hit land. They are a danger to people's lives. They can also do billions of dollars of damage to homes and businesses. Strong construction is needed. For this challenge, imagine you have been hired to help cities impacted by hurricanes. You will build a structure (home or building) that can stand up to a hurricane.

Criteria

For the design to be successful, it must…

- remain standing and intact under wind speeds from a fan.
- remain standing and intact when sprayed with water.
- be at least 10 inches (25 cm) tall.

Constraint

- You may only use the materials provided to you.

My Summary

_____

_____

_____

_____

My Questions

_____

_____

_____

_____

Unit 10: Hurricanes

Name: _____ Date: _____

Directions: Research how communities are affected by hurricanes, and answer the questions. Then, brainstorm and record ideas for your structure. Discuss ideas with others, and add to your brainstorming.

1. What types of damage can hurricanes cause? Give two examples from your research.

   _____

   _____

   _____

2. What types of special features do buildings in hurricane states have?

   _____

   _____

3. How do people prepare their homes when they know a hurricane is coming?

   _____

   _____

My Brainstorming

_____

_____

_____

_____

_____

_____

_____

_____

Name: _____ **Date:** _____

Directions: Sketch one or more designs for your hurricane-proof structure. List the materials.

[ ]

Materials

_____   _____   _____

_____   _____   _____

 Think About It!

What will keep your structure from blowing over? How will your structure react to getting wet?

Unit 10: Hurricanes

Name: _____ Date: _____

Directions: Gather your materials, plan your steps, and build your hurricane-proof structure. Record notes as you build.

Hurricane Structure Building Plan

	Job or Task	Group Member(s)
1		
2		
3		
4		
5		
6		

Building Notes
(additional steps, problems, adjustments, etc.)

Name: _____ Date: _____

Directions: Read the notes about setting up and completing the test. Test your structure by imitating a hurricane. Record the results.

Testing Notes

- You may not touch the structure during the test. If the structure attaches to something, you may hold that in place.
- If the structure falls over, you may stand it back up before beginning the next category test.
- Place the fan 2 feet (61 cm) from the structure.
- Spray the water 1 foot (30 cm) from the structure.

Testing Conditions	Structure's Reaction to Wind	Structure's Reaction to Water
Category 1 Hurricane (fan on low setting for 10 seconds and five sprays with the water bottle)		
Category 3 Hurricane (fan on medium setting for 10 seconds and five more sprays with the water bottle)		
Category 5 Hurricane (fan on high setting for 10 seconds and five more sprays with the water bottle)		

Day 1

Name: _____ Date: _____

Directions: Reflect on your design, and answer the questions. Then, plan how you will improve it. Conduct additional research if needed.

1. What parts and materials in your first structure worked well?

_____

_____

_____

2. What could make the structure design even better?

_____

_____

_____

Draw a star next to one or more ways you will improve your design.

- My first design did not meet all the criteria. To improve it, I will

_____

_____

- Make the structure taller. It will be _____ inches tall.

- My own idea: _____

_____

Name: _____ **Date:** _____

Directions: Plan and sketch your new hurricane-proof structure design. Circle the parts that are new or different. Label the materials you will use for each part. Then, complete the sentence.

In my redesign, I will...

add _____

remove _____

change _____

1. The change or improvement I think is most important is _____

_____

_____

Unit 10: Hurricanes

Name: _____ Date: _____

Directions: Gather your materials, answer the question, and plan your steps. Rebuild your hurricane-proof structure. Record notes as you build.

1. What did you learn from building the first design that you can apply as you rebuild?

   _____

   _____

Hurricane Structure Rebuilding Plan

	Job or Task	Group Member(s)
1		
2		
3		
4		
5		
6		

Building Notes
(additional steps, surprises, changes, etc.)

Name: _____ **Date:** _____

Directions: Read the notes about setting up and completing the test. Test your structure by imitating a hurricane. Record the results.

Testing Notes

- You may not touch the structure during the test. If the structure attaches to something, you may hold that in place.
- If the structure falls over, you may stand it back up before beginning the next category test.
- Place the fan 2 feet (61 cm) from the structure.
- Spray the water 1 foot (30 cm) from the structure.

Testing Conditions	Structure's Reaction to Wind	Structure's Reaction to Water
Category 1 Hurricane (fan on low setting for 10 seconds and five sprays with the water bottle)		
Category 3 Hurricane (fan on medium setting for 10 seconds and five more sprays with the water bottle)		
Category 5 Hurricane (fan on high setting for 10 seconds and five more sprays with the water bottle)		

Name: _____ Date: _____

Directions: Answer the questions to reflect on your structure.

1. Which structure had more success? What is your evidence?

   _____

   _____

2. If you could build the structure again, what changes would you make to the materials or design? Explain your reasoning.

   _____

   _____

   _____

3. How do you think buildings in hurricane states should be built to stay safe during hurricanes?

   _____

   _____

   _____

4. Draw yourself testing your design. Add a thought bubble or speech bubble. Write a caption telling what you are doing.

Sun and Stars Teaching Support

Overview of Unit Activities

Students will learn about and explore the sun and stars through the following activities:

- reading about the Milky Way
- studying a graphic about comets
- experimenting with how light pollution affects seeing stars
- creating drawings showing perspective
- comparing the sizes of the planets
- building and launching bottle rockets

Materials Per Group

Week 1

- basic school supplies
- black construction paper
- dark room
- flashlight

STEAM Challenge

- air pump and needle
- baking soda
- basic school supplies
- books or online resources about real rockets and bottle rockets
- cardboard sheets (3–4)
- construction paper
- corks that fit in the mouths of the 2-liter bottles (can be bought online; wadded up paper towels can also be used)
- duct and/or masking tape
- measuring tape or stick
- paint
- plastic bottles (various sizes, including 2-liter)
- poster board
- stopwatch
- straws (5–10)
- vinegar
- water

Setup and Instructional Tips

- **STEAM Challenge:** The challenge can be done individually or in groups. Students working in groups should sketch their own designs first. Then, have them share designs in groups and choose one together.

- **Testing Days:** Use safety glasses when launching the rocket. Make sure there is ample space between the students and the launching rockets. Keep students out of the way when the rockets fall to the ground.

Discussion Questions

- What is in the solar system?
- What is a galaxy?
- Why do stars seem to be different sizes and brightnesses?
- Why do you think scientists are interested in learning about space?

Additional Notes

- **Possible Misconception:** The sun is bigger and brighter than other stars.
  Truth: The sun seems big and bright because it is closer to Earth than other stars.

- **Possible Design Solutions:** Methods for launching might include putting water in the bottom of a bottle, attaching a bike pump needle, and pressing the pump for launch. Putting vinegar in bottles, adding baking soda, and shaking bottles will cause a chemical reaction that increases air pressure and will push out corks, causing rockets to launch. Students might add enhancements to their bottles, such as fins to the bottoms or sides, or cones to the top. Students may create simple launchpads to balance the bottles while they launch.

Scaffolding and Extension Suggestions

- Use concentric circles to help students understand Earth's location (Earth is in the solar system; in the Milky Way galaxy; in the universe).

- Challenge students to investigate terms such as *black hole*, *Goldilocks zone*, and *big bang theory* to increase their knowledge of space and share with the class.

Answer Key

Week 1 Day 1
1. B
2. A
3. D
4. C

Week 1 Day 2
1. 1986
2. The nucleus is the center, and the coma is the gas that surrounds the nucleus.
3. A comet has a tail because the sun's heat turns some of the nucleus into gas which streaks behind the comet.

Week 1 Day 5
1. Venus
2. Mercury, Mars, Venus, Earth, Neptune, Uranus, Saturn, Jupiter
3. Responses should include things that students found surprising about sizes of planets

Weeks 2 & 3
See STEAM Challenge Rubric on page 221.

Name: _____ Date: _____

Directions: Read the text, and choose the best answer for each question.

The Milky Way

The sun, Earth, and other planets and their moons make up our solar system. Asteroids and meteors are also in it. Asteroids are small, rocky bodies that revolve around a star. Meteors are pieces of rock or metal that fall from space into Earth's atmosphere. But our solar system is just a small part of the Milky Way galaxy. A galaxy is a system of stars held together by gravity. The Milky Way has hundreds of billions of stars. That's a lot! Each of those stars can have planets that revolve around them. A black hole is at the center of the galaxy. Scientists continue to study the Milky Way and often learn new information.

sun

---

1. What holds a galaxy together?

   Ⓐ stars

   Ⓑ gravity

   Ⓒ black holes

   Ⓓ asteroids

2. What does an asteroid revolve around?

   Ⓐ a star

   Ⓑ a planet

   Ⓒ a galaxy

   Ⓓ a moon

3. What is at the center of the Milky Way galaxy?

   Ⓐ a meteor

   Ⓑ a star

   Ⓒ a planet

   Ⓓ a black hole

4. Which of these could be in Earth's atmosphere?

   Ⓐ black hole

   Ⓑ asteroid

   Ⓒ meteor

   Ⓓ star

Name: _____ Date: _____

Directions: Read the text, and study the diagram. Then, answer the questions.

Comets

Comets are objects in space made of icy rock that revolve around the sun. During their travel, they get very close to the sun. This makes part of the ice melt and turn to gas. A long, glowing tail appears. Halley's Comet passes by Earth about every 76 years. The next time it will be visible is in the year 2062.

coma—the thin atmosphere of gas that surrounds a comet's nucleus

tail—the streak of gas and dust behind a comet

nucleus—icy, rocky center of a comet

1. When was the last time Halley's Comet was visible on Earth?

_____

2. What is the difference between the nucleus and the coma of a comet?

_____

_____

3. Why does a comet have a tail?

_____

_____

Name: _____ Date: _____

Directions: Follow the steps to investigate how light pollution affects the appearance of stars.

> **Question:** How does light pollution affect stargazing?

Materials		
construction paper	dark room	flashlight
pencil	tape	

Steps

1. Cut a piece of construction paper a little larger than the face of the flashlight.

2. Use a pencil to poke holes in the construction paper to make stars. Tape it to the face of the flashlight.

3. Make the room as dark as possible (turn off lights, close blinds, block cracks under the door, etc.)

4. Shine the flashlight on the ceiling and observe.

5. Keep the flashlight on, and slowly make the room brighter.

6. Observe what happens to the appearance of the stars.

> Light pollution is when the night sky is brighter than it should be because of human-made lights.

 Talk About It!

> What did you see when the room was dark? What happened as light was added back to the room? How could light pollution affect people and animals?

Name: _____ Date: _____

Day 4

Directions: Read the text about perspective, and study the example. Then, create a drawing that uses perspective to make something small seem big.

The sun is a star, but it looks bigger and brighter than the nighttime stars. It isn't, though. It is just closer than the others. A closer object will often look larger than objects in the distance. In the example, all the ladders would be the same size in real life. But the one in front looks larger because it is closer.

Name: _____ Date: _____

Directions: Study the diagram and table. Then, answer the questions.

Diameters of the Planets in Our Solar System

Planet	Diameter (in km)
Mercury	4,879
Venus	12,104
Earth	12,756
Mars	6,779
Jupiter	142,800
Saturn	120,660
Uranus	51,118
Neptune	49,528

*Diameter is the distance through the center of a circle from one side to the other.

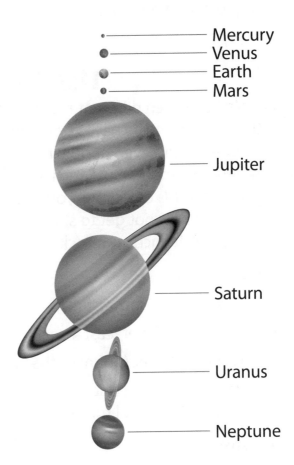

Mercury
Venus
Earth
Mars

Jupiter

Saturn

Uranus

Neptune

1. Which planet is closest in size to Earth? _____

2. Write the planets in size order starting with the smallest.

   _____

   _____

   _____

3. What surprised you about the size of the planets?

   _____

   _____

   _____

Name: _____ Date: _____

Directions: Read the text. Then, summarize the challenge in your own words. Write any questions you have.

The Challenge

People have used different methods to study space for centuries. In the last 100 years, scientists have been able to learn about space in new ways. Ships, cameras, and even people have traveled beyond Earth to learn about the mysteries of space. Rockets have the big power for sending something into space. For this challenge, you will create a bottle rocket and a method to launch it. It may not get to space, but it will still be fun and educational! Your group will launch your rocket and collect data.

Criteria

For the design to be successful, it must…

- stay airborne for at least 4 seconds.
- land within 5 feet (1.5 m) of the launch location.
- have one or more structures on the outside of the bottle to help it look and move like a real rocket.

Constraints

- You may only use the materials provided to you.
- You may only use one plastic bottle in your first design.

My Summary

_____

_____

_____

My Questions

_____

_____

_____

Day 2

Name: _____ **Date:** _____

Directions: Research rockets and how to make a bottle rocket. Then, answer the questions based on your findings. Brainstorm and record ideas. Discuss ideas with others, and add to your brainstorming.

1. What is the purpose of a rocket when launching a spaceship?

   _____

   _____

2. What is a way to launch a bottle rocket with an air pump?

   _____

   _____

3. What is a way to launch a bottle rocket with vinegar and baking soda?

   _____

   _____

4. What methods or design ideas did you discover about building and launching bottle rockets?

   _____

   _____

My Brainstorming

_____

_____

_____

_____

_____

_____

_____

Name: _____ Date: _____

Directions: Sketch one or more designs for your bottle rocket. Label the parts, and list the materials you will need to build and launch your rocket. Then, answer the question.

Materials

_____   _____   _____

_____   _____   _____

1. How will you launch your rocket?

_____

_____

Unit 11: Sun and Stars

Week 2

Day 4

Name: _____ Date: _____

Directions: Gather your materials, plan your steps, and build your bottle rocket. Then, answer the questions about launching your rocket.

Bottle Rocket Building Plan

	Job or Task	Group Member(s)
1		
2		
3		
4		
5		
6		

1. What steps will you follow to launch your rocket?

- _____
- _____
- _____
- _____
- _____

2. What can you do to extend the rocket's airtime?

_____

_____

_____

3. How can you make the rocket land close to the launch pad?

_____

_____

_____

Unit 11: Sun and Stars

Name: _____ Date: _____

Directions: Set up your bottle rocket outside. Put on safety goggles, and make sure the area is clear. Follow your steps to launch your bottle rocket. Time how long it stays in the air. Measure how far away it lands. Record the results, and draw and write your observations during the launch. Then, answer the question.

Launch Results	
Time in the Air	
Landing Distance	

My Observations

1. Would you consider this launch to be a success? Why or why not?

_____

_____

_____

Name: _____ Date: _____

Directions: Reflect on your design, and answer the questions. Then, plan how you will improve it. Conduct additional research if needed.

1. What went well with the bottle rocket design and launch?

_____

_____

_____

2. What could make the rocket go higher?

_____

_____

_____

3. What changes might help the rocket stay closer to the launch location?

_____

_____

_____

_____

The following constraint has been changed:

- You may use any number or size of plastic bottles.

4. How could the constraint change help your rocket design?

_____

_____

_____

Day 2

Name: _____ Date: _____

Directions: Plan and sketch your new bottle rocket design. Label the parts and the materials you will use for each part. Then, complete the sentence.

In my redesign, I will…

add _____

remove _____

change _____

1. I think this design will work better because _____

_____

_____

Name: _____ Date: _____

Directions: Gather your materials, plan your steps, and rebuild your bottle rocket. Then, answer the questions about launching your rocket.

Bottle Rocket Rebuilding Plan

	Job or Task	Group Member(s)
1		
2		
3		
4		
5		
6		

1. What steps will you follow to launch your new rocket?

- _____
- _____
- _____
- _____
- _____

2. What can you do to extend the rocket's airtime even more?

_____

_____

_____

3. How can you make the rocket land closer to the launch pad?

_____

_____

_____

Day 4

Name: _____ Date: _____

Directions: Set up your bottle rocket outside. Put on safety goggles, and make sure the area is clear. Follow your steps to launch your bottle rocket. Time how long it stays in the air. Measure how far away it lands. Record the results, and draw and write your observations during the launch. Then, answer the question.

Launch Results	
Time in the Air	
Landing Distance	

My Observations

1. Did your new bottle rocket design perform better? What is your evidence and reasoning?

_____

_____

_____

Day 5

Name: _____ Date: _____

Directions: Answer the questions to reflect on your bottle rocket.

1. Which launch would you consider to be more successful? Explain your answer.

   _____

   _____

2. What was the biggest problem you faced making your rocket?

   _____

   _____

3. How would you compare your rocket launch to a space rocket launch?

   _____

   _____

4. Draw yourself as an astronaut launching into space in a NASA space shuttle. Add a thought bubble or speech bubble. Write a caption telling what you are doing.

Water on Earth Teaching Support

Overview of Unit Activities

Students will learn about and explore water on Earth through the following activities:

- reading about water on Earth
- reading about polar ice caps and glaciers
- experimenting with the densities of fresh and salt water
- creating paintings with watercolors and salt
- using a graph about water sources
- creating aqueducts that transport water from one place to another

Materials Per Group

Week 1

- basic school supplies
- cups (2)
- hardboiled egg
- paintbrush
- salt (4 tsp., 24 g)

- small objects of differing densities (carrot sticks, bars of soap, etc.)
- water
- watercolor paper (optional)
- watercolors

STEAM Challenge

- basic school supplies
- books, boxes, or furniture (for height)
- books or online resources about aqueducts
- cardboard sheets (3–4)
- cardboard tubes (5–10)
- craft sticks (10–20)
- foil

- ice cubes
- masking or duct tape
- plastic wrap (for waterproofing)
- poster board
- shallow bowls or plates with a lip
- tarp (optional)
- water

Setup and Instructional Tips

- **STEAM Challenge:** The challenge can be done individually or in groups. Students working in groups should sketch their own designs first. Then, have them share designs in groups and choose one together.

- **Testing Days:** Conduct the aqueduct tests outdoors if possible. If it is done inside, put down a tarp. Be sure to clean up any spills indoors.

Discussion Questions

- What is the difference between salt water and fresh water?
- Where can different types of water be found?
- Why is water pollution dangerous?
- What water can people drink?

Additional Notes

- **Possible Misconception:** The water people drink is new.
  Truth: There is no new water on Earth—it has gone through the water cycle countless times.
- **Possible Design Solutions:** Students may use cardboard to make traditional aqueducts that support themselves, or they may build chute-style aqueducts with supports (see illustrations). To create the height for the water source, students may stack books or boxes or place them on chairs or crates.

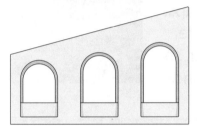 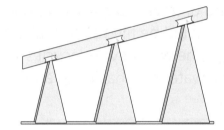

Scaffolding and Extension Suggestions

- Show students maps or globes of the Earth to allow students to see how much of it is covered in water.
- Challenge students to model their aqueducts after ancient Roman structures.

Answer Key

Week 1 Day 1
1. C
2. B
3. D
4. A

Week 1 Day 2
1. Glaciers move down a slope because of gravity and their weight.
2. Example: Scientists might study glacial ice because it can be hundreds of thousands of years old. By learning about the ice, they can learn about the past.

Week 1 Day 5
1. 3 percent
2. Water deep in the Earth is unusable because scientists cannot get to it, or it might be very expensive to get it.

Weeks 2 & 3
See STEAM Challenge Rubric on page 221.

Name: _____ Date: _____

Directions: Read the text, and choose the best answer for each question.

Water on Earth

Over 70 percent of Earth's surface is water. Almost all of that is ocean water. The ocean is beautiful and full of interesting creatures. But people cannot really use the salty water. It cannot be easily used to drink or water crops. People need fresh water for that. Fresh water is found in lakes, rivers, and streams. A reservoir is a natural or human-made lake that stores fresh water. Fresh water can also be found underground or frozen in glaciers and ice caps. Fresh water should be filtered to make it safe for drinking. The water cycle recycles water, so people drink water that has been around since Earth began!

1. What covers the majority of Earth?
   - (A) land
   - (B) fresh water
   - (C) oceans
   - (D) glaciers

2. A _____ stores water.
   - (A) glacier
   - (B) reservoir
   - (C) stream
   - (D) filter

3. Where is fresh water *not* found?
   - (A) stream
   - (B) glacier
   - (C) lake
   - (D) ocean

4. What type of water should be used to water crops?
   - (A) fresh water
   - (B) salt water
   - (C) ocean water
   - (D) frozen water

Name: _____ **Date:** _____

Directions: Study the web, and answer the questions.

```
        ┌──────────────┐
        │  most are in │
        │ Antarctica and│
        │   Greenland  │
        └──────────────┘

┌──────────┐              ┌──────────────┐
│fresh water│             │ almost 200,000│
└──────────┘              │   on Earth    │
                          └──────────────┘

    ┌────────────────────────────────────────┐
    │ glacier—a body of ice that starts on land│
    │ and slowly moves down a slope because of  │
    │ gravity and its weight                    │
    └────────────────────────────────────────┘

┌──────────────────┐        ┌──────────────────┐
│ glacial ice can be│       │  made of snow that│
│hundreds of thousands│     │hardens into ice over time│
│   of years old    │       └──────────────────┘
└──────────────────┘
```

1. Why do glaciers move?

_____

_____

_____

2. Why do you think scientists study glacial ice?

_____

_____

_____

Name: _____ Date: _____

Directions: Follow the steps to complete an activity about salt water and fresh water.

> **Question:** Can items float in fresh water or salt water?

Materials			
2 cups	carrot stick	egg	measuring spoon
other small objects	salt	soap bar	water

Steps

1. Fill two cups a little more than halfway with water.

2. Add 4 tablespoons (71 g) of salt to one of the cups and stir until it dissolves.

3. Place an egg into the fresh water. Then place it into the salt water.

4. Repeat with soap, a carrot stick, or other small objects.

What Is Happening?

Adding salt to the water gives it more mass. This increases its density. If an object has less density than the water, it will float. If an object has more density than the water, it will sink.

Talk About It!

Which cup of water did the egg float in? Why?

How could salt water affect animals swimming in the ocean?

If a small object sinks in water, how could you get it to float?

Day 4

Name: _____ **Date:** _____

Directions: Create a painting using watercolors and salt! Paint a design or pattern using watercolors in the space below. Be sure the paint is very watery. Sprinkle salt on the wet paint. Watch your beautiful design emerge as it dries.

Unit 12: Water on Earth

Name: _____ Date: _____

Directions: Study the graph, and read the information. Then, answer the questions.

Water on Earth

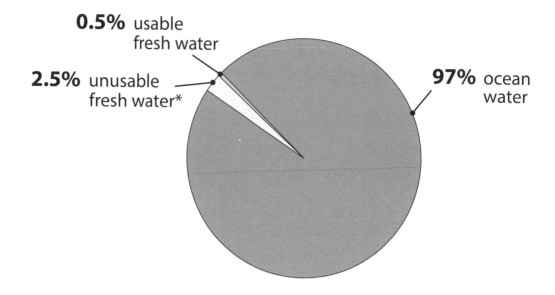

0.5% usable fresh water

2.5% unusable fresh water*

97% ocean water

*Fresh water can be unusable for many reasons. It might be stored in glaciers or ice caps, or it might be very deep underground. Some fresh water is in the atmosphere. And sadly, some fresh water is too polluted to use.

1. What percentage of Earth's water is not ocean?

   _____

2. Why would water deep underground be considered unusable?

   _____

   _____

3. How does this information relate to water conservation?

   _____

   _____

   _____

Day 1

Name: _____ **Date:** _____

Directions: Read the text. Then, summarize the challenge in your own words. Write any questions you have.

The Challenge

Thousands of years ago, living near fresh water was ideal. But it wasn't always possible. So, people built aqueducts. These structures looked like bridges, but they were channels designed to carry water from the source to where people needed it. Technology has changed a lot since those days. But aqueducts are still used in some parts of the world.

Imagine a new community is far from fresh water. Its people need to get water from a reservoir atop a mountain to their homes. For this challenge, you must create an aqueduct that can transport water from one place to another.

Criteria

For the design to be successful, it must…

- move water from one place to another, at least 3 feet (91 cm) apart.

- empty water into a shallow bowl without splashing.

Constraints

- You may only use the materials provided to you.

- The water at the beginning of the aqueduct should be 2 feet (61 cm) off of the ground (to simulate the mountain elevation).

My Summary

_____

_____

_____

My Questions

_____

_____

_____

Unit 12: Water on Earth

Name: _____ Date: _____

Directions: Research aqueducts, and answer the questions. Then, brainstorm and record ideas. Discuss ideas with others, and add to your brainstorming.

1. What is an aqueduct?

_____

_____

2. What is an advantage and a disadvantage of having an aqueduct?

_____

_____

3. What are some examples of what aqueducts look like? Draw one or more examples.

My Brainstorming

Name: _____ Date: _____

Directions: Sketch one or more designs for your aqueduct. Show where the water source will be and how the water will flow. List the materials. Then, answer the question.

Materials

_____   _____   _____

_____   _____   _____

Think About It!

Will your aqueduct have enough support? What will happen if the water flows too fast?

Unit 12: Water on Earth

Name: _____ Date: _____

Directions: Gather your materials, plan your steps, and build your aqueduct. Make sure all the parts are secure. Record notes as you build.

Aqueduct Building Plan

	Job or Task	Group Member(s)
1		
2		
3		
4		
5		
6		

Building Notes
(additional steps, problems, changes, etc.)

Name: _____ **Date:** _____

Directions: Set up your aqueduct on a flat surface. Measure the height of the starting point of your aqueduct. Pour 2 cups (500 mL) of water into the aqueduct at the starting point. Watch as the water is carried by the aqueduct. Record your observations before, during, and after testing.

Before	Is the starting point of the aqueduct 2 feet (61 cm) high? yes no Is the aqueduct secure? yes no Is the bowl set up to catch the water? yes no What else do you notice? _____ _____ _____
During	What do you observe as the water flows along the aqueduct? Draw or write what you see.
After	Did water splash out of the bowl? yes no If yes, describe how much. _____ Can the aqueduct still carry water? yes no What else do you notice? _____ _____ _____

Unit 12: Water on Earth

Day 1

Name: _____ Date: _____

Directions: Reflect on your design, and answer the questions. Then, plan how you will improve it. Conduct additional research if needed.

1. What went well with your first aqueduct design?

   _____

   _____

   _____

2. What changes do you need to make for it to work better?

   _____

   _____

   _____

The following constraint for the challenge has changed:

- The starting point of the aqueduct should begin at a height of 3 feet (91 cm).

3. How will the height of the starting point affect the water's speed?

   _____

   _____

   _____

4. What adjustments will you need to make on your aqueduct to make sure water doesn't splash out of the bowl?

   _____

   _____

   _____

Name: _____ Date: _____

Directions: Plan and sketch your new aqueduct design. Label the parts and the materials you will use for each part. Then, complete the sentence.

In my redesign, I will...

add _____

remove _____

change _____

1. The change or improvement I am most excited about is _____

_____

_____

Name: _____ Date: _____

Directions: Gather your materials, plan your steps, and rebuild your aqueduct. Make sure all the parts are secure. Record notes as you build.

Aqueduct Rebuilding Plan

	Job or Task	Group Member(s)
1		
2		
3		
4		
5		
6		

Building Notes
(challenges, solutions, observations, etc.)

Name: _____ Date: _____

Directions: Set up your aqueduct on a flat surface. Measure the height of the starting point of your aqueduct. Pour 2 cups (500 mL) of water into the aqueduct at the starting point. Watch as the water is carried by the aqueduct. Record your observations before, during, and after testing.

Before	Is the starting point of the aqueduct 3 feet (91 cm) high? yes no Is the aqueduct secure? yes no Is the bowl set up to catch the water? yes no What else do you notice? _____ _____ _____
During	What do you observe as the water flows along the aqueduct? Draw or write what you see.
After	Did water splash out of the bowl? yes no If yes, describe how much. _____ Can the aqueduct still carry water? yes no What else do you notice? _____ _____ _____

Unit 12: Water on Earth

Name: _____ Date: _____

Directions: Answer the questions to reflect on your aqueduct.

1. What surprises you about aqueducts from the past?

   _____

   _____

   _____

2. Could an aqueduct help any community that is not near a fresh water source? Explain your answer.

   _____

   _____

   _____

3. What advice would you give to someone building an aqueduct?

   _____

   _____

   _____

4. What did you enjoy most about this challenge?

   _____

   _____

   _____

Name: _____ Date: _____

STEAM Challenge Rubric

Directions: Think about the challenge. Score each item on a scale of 3 to 1. Circle your score.

	3	2	1
Criteria	The final design was successful in meeting the goals. Or major improvements were made through logical, evidence-based design changes.	The final design was partially successful in meeting the goals. Attempts to improve the design were partially successful.	The final project was not successful in meeting the goals. Attempts were not thoughtful or based on research.
Constraints	All instructions for the challenge were followed. The final design was completed within the constraints given.	Some instructions for the challenge were followed. The final design was partially completed within the constraints given.	Instructions for the challenge were not followed. No consideration for constraints was made.
Group Collaboration	Students cooperated to complete the project. Students divided work fairly. Students accepted and learned from each other's mistakes and worked together to find solutions. There was consistently calm communication.	Work was divided fairly among group members for the most part. Group members were sometimes supportive or helpful in problem-solving. Students struggled to compromise but found ways to work together.	Work was not divided fairly. Group members were not supportive of mistakes nor helpful in problem-solving. Heated disagreements occurred and/or compromises could not be reached.
Creativity	Students applied their knowledge in several unique ways to solve problems. New and innovative approaches to the problem were tested.	Students applied their knowledge in one unique way. At least one innovative approach to the problem was tested.	Students did not attempt any unique solutions to the problem. Innovative approaches were not tested.

Student Score: _____   Teacher Score: _____

Name: _____ Date: _____

Summative Assessment

Directions: Read the questions. Write the answers on a separate sheet of paper.

1. Which of these is a definition of *constraints*?

   (A) the goals of a project

   (B) when someone says something is unacceptable

   (C) limits or restrictions for a project

   (D) something that is too small to be seen without a microscope

2. Which of these is an example of a constraint?

   (A) To be considered a success, your rocket must fly to a height of at least 100 meters.

   (B) You may not use any food items to build your rocket.

   (C) Most rockets make use of Newton's 2nd Law of Motion.

   (D) You have been hired to design and build a model rocket.

3. Which of these is an example of a criterion?

   (A) To be considered a success, your rocket must fly to a height of at least 100 meters.

   (B) You may not use any food items to build your rocket.

   (C) Most rockets make use of Newton's 2nd Law of Motion.

   (D) You have been hired to design and build a model rocket.

4. During which stage of the engineering design process do you look for examples of successful solutions to similar problems?

   (A) Research and Brainstorm

   (B) Plan and Design

   (C) Build and Create

   (D) Test and Evaluate

5. Why is research part of the engineering design process?

6. Scientist and author Isaac Asimov once said, "Science can amuse and fascinate us all, but it is engineering that changes the world." What do you think he meant? Do agree with his statement?

7. A friend of yours just finished building a swing. What would you advise them to do next?

Engineering Design Process

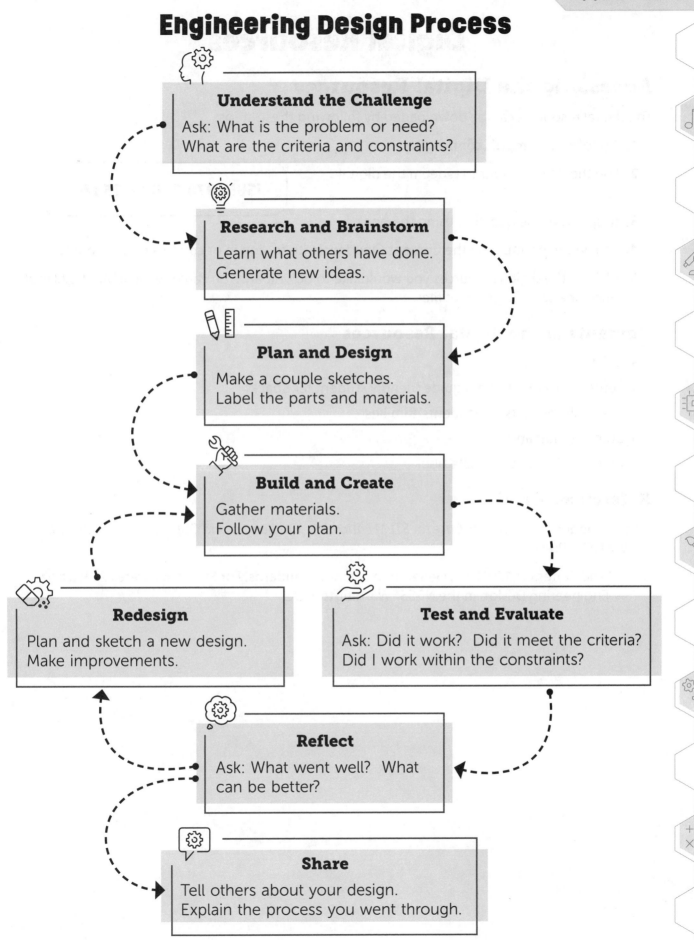

Understand the Challenge

Ask: What is the problem or need?
What are the criteria and constraints?

Research and Brainstorm

Learn what others have done.
Generate new ideas.

Plan and Design

Make a couple sketches.
Label the parts and materials.

Build and Create

Gather materials.
Follow your plan.

Redesign

Plan and sketch a new design.
Make improvements.

Test and Evaluate

Ask: Did it work? Did it meet the criteria?
Did I work within the constraints?

Reflect

Ask: What went well? What can be better?

Share

Tell others about your design.
Explain the process you went through.

Digital Resources

Accessing the Digital Resources

The digital resources can be downloaded by following these steps:

1. Go to **www.tcmpub.com/digital**.

2. Use the ISBN number to redeem the digital resources.

3. Respond to the question using the book.

4. Follow the prompts on the Content Cloud website to sign in or create a new account.

5. Choose the digital resources you would like to download. You can download all the files at once or a specific group of files.

ISBN: 978-1-4258-2532-4

Contents of the Digital Resources

- Safety Contract
- Sentence frames to help guide friendly student feedback
- Materials requests for students' families
- Student Glossary
- Materials list for the whole book

References Cited

Bybee, Rodger W. 2013. *The Case for STEM Education: Challenges and Opportunities.* Arlington, VA: NSTA Press.

NGSS Lead States. 2013. "Next Generation Science Standards: For States, By States APPENDIX I—Engineering Design in the NGSS." Washington, DC.